D0463796

It Happened In Series

IT HAPPENED IN
NORTH
CAROLINA

Scotti Kent

TWODOT®

GUILFORD, CONNECTICUT
HELENA, MONTANA
AN IMPRINT OF THE GLOBE PEQUOT PRESS

To my son, Ryan, and daughter, Brynna—because they both "happened" in North Carolina!

A · TWODOT · BOOK

Copyright © 2000 Morris Book Publishing, LLC
Previously published by Falcon® Publishing, Inc.

TwoDot is a registered trademark of Morris Book Publishing, LLC.

Cover art © 2000 Lisa Harvey

Library of Congress Cataloging-in-Publication Data
Kent, Scotti, 1950-
    It happened in North Carolina / Scotti Kent.
        p. cm.
    Includes bibliographical references and index.
    ISBN 978-1-56044-966-9
    1. North Carolina—History—Anecdotes. I. Title.
F254.6.K46 2000
975.6—dc21   00-032575

Printed in the United States of America.
First Edition/Fifth Printing

Contents

Poskito

· 1250 ·

It was late summer in the Pee Dee River Valley in North Carolina's southern piedmont region. The year could have been 1250 or 1346 or any one of the more than two hundred years during which the area was hunted, fished, and farmed by a tribe archaeologists later named the Pee Dee Indians.

Corn stalks stood tall and proud in the fields, shimmering bright green in the summer sun. In every village people turned their attention to Poskito: the most important event of the year. Each little brown hut was cleaned thoroughly, its floors swept and sprinkled with fresh sand. Old clothing, pottery, and implements were replaced with new. Debts and grievances were settled. Unpunished crimes, except for murder, were forgiven. All hearth fires were extinguished.

At the appointed time, the villagers abandoned their stickball games, basketmaking, and hunting and made their way to a low bluff overlooking the juncture of the Little River and Town Fork Creek. There they joined other tribe members inside an oval-shaped stockade made from closely set posts driven into the ground. The stockade fence was interwoven with cane and small poles and plastered with a mixture of clay and straw. Within the enclosure was a large open plaza that served as a public meeting place.

Today, archaeologists consider the Pee Dee culture part of a widespread tradition known as South Appalachian Mississippian. Town Creek, as their complex society's hub eventually came to be called, was located in what is now Montgomery County, North

Carolina. It was a regional center that interacted and evolved with other regional centers across the Coastal Plain of Georgia and South Carolina to the western North Carolina mountains.

At one end of the Town Creek plaza, in a square compound next to the river, stood the minor temple where the priests lived. Like all ceremonial structures, it was rectangular with a thatched roof. Its walls were made of upright stakes bound together with strong, flexible willow twigs, then covered in mud.

Around the edge of the public area were small, round huts, some of which contained the graves of loved ones who had died from injury, disease, or old age. A game pole stood in the center of the plaza, the skull of a bear hanging from its top. Many a warrior distinguished himself in competition during strenuous ball games in which strength and courage were put to the test.

Across from the priests' dwelling rose a pyramid-shaped mound, about ten feet wide and five feet high. On top sat the structure that served as a major temple, council house, and lodge.

More than once in years past, the temple had been destroyed by violent storms and heavy rains. At one point the elders decided to elevate the place of worship so that it would be nearer to their sun god. For many months the men, women, and children of the tribe who were not needed elsewhere spent their days digging clay out of lowland pits with sharp-pointed sticks. They carried the clay in baskets to the site where the remains of the old temples lay. By packing the clay along the edge of a large square, they built a rim, then filled it in. On top of this mound they built a rectangular structure from logs and sod and a ramp that led from the top of the platform down into the village.

The project was a major undertaking, but the villagers were accustomed to hard work. It was not in their nature to give up. Around A.D. 1200 their ancestors had traveled a long distance over stony ground, through dense undergrowth, across swamps and hazardous waterways to find this paradise on earth, with its fertile fields and abundant game. They had defended their new home from marauders and weathered the ravages of disease. The effort required to construct the mound and new temple seemed slight by comparison.

By late summer, everything was ready for Poskito. The *Town Creek Indian Mound Guidebook* offers the following description:

> The Poskito, or renewal ceremony, was the most important of several ceremonies to be held in the square ground during the year. Known by the white man as the ceremony of the "busk," deriving from the Indian word meaning "a fast," it also was referred to as the "green corn ceremony," as corn played an important part in the ritual performed. The eight day celebration was held after the gathering of the first new corn crop, to mark the beginning of the new year. . . . During the first four days of the busk, people from the surrounding villages gathered at the Town Creek ceremonial center to take part in rituals of purification. These included ceremonial bathing, fasting, scratching the body with a gar fish tooth or sharp stone to expel evil spirits, and taking cathartic medicines. The most famous of these medicines, the black drink, was made from the leaves of the yaupon shrub. After the leaves were parched in pots and then steeped in boiling water, the resultant black liquid was served to participants in whom it induced violent vomiting, thus cleansing the individual of inner evil.

The second half of the Poskito was much more enjoyable. First, the sacred fire was rekindled. Ears of new corn were offered to the spirits and the people themselves were allowed to partake of the fruits of their labor. The young men of the tribe who had proven their manhood that year were given warrior names. After a period of feasting and celebrating, the participants took embers from the new fire back to their villages to relight the hearths in their homes, ensuring that they would remain "the people of one fire."

The Pee Dee Indians did not write down the story of the busk for future generations to read, but they left something even more valuable than written documents: their own remains and the discarded objects of their everyday lives. As historian Joffre L. Coe wrote in his book *Town Creek Indian Mound*, their story

> is not a book that can be read in an easy chair in the comfort of home, but it is a book whose pages must be carefully turned with the shovel and the trowel in the hot sun and in the rain. . . . The reading is hard, the story is incomplete, but that which is learned gives us a better understanding of those who have gone before.

Each year, Pee Dee villagers not only renewed their lives through the Poskito ceremony, they also left signs and symbols of their existence in the earth beneath their feet. In doing so they provided proof that long before Europeans first spotted the shores of North Carolina, the "people of one fire" called it home.

The Roanoke Colony
· 1590 ·

John White shifted his weight to keep from losing his balance as the *Hopewell* lurched forward, overcoming yet another wave. The planks beneath his feet groaned and choppy foam sloshed against the ship's hull. Squinting into the salt breeze, White curled his hands a little tighter around the weathered rail. Although the ocean seemed quiet at the moment, the storms of the past ten days were fresh in his mind. He cringed as he recalled the driving rain, deafening explosions of thunder, and great churning spouts of water. More than once he had expected to be washed overboard.

But today the weather was calm, and the *Hopewell* plowed steadily and confidently through the swells. Off the starboard bow White caught sight of the *Hopewell*'s companion ship, the *Moonlight*, in full sail. His gaze shifted to a strip of land in the distance, which he recognized as the Island of Croatoan. Just beyond it lay the newfound land—a place White called "Virginia," now part of the state of North Carolina. Over the past three years White had often wondered if he would ever see this place again.

In August of 1587, he had left the New World for England to gather provisions for the men, women, and children of Sir Walter Raleigh's Virginia settlement. He planned to return within a matter of months. About the same time, however, the English learned that Phillip II of Spain was sending the Spanish Armada their way. Queen Elizabeth ordered all ships to stand by in preparation for war.

White persisted. In the spring of 1588, he was granted the use of two small vessels not suited for battle against Spain. They set sail on April 22, but one month after their departure, the English ships limped home, crippled from an encounter with the French. White hoped to set out for Virginia again that summer, but renewed threats from Spain forced him to cancel his plans.

Time slipped away. Finally, with the help of several London merchants, White secured passage on the *Hopewell*, which set sail in March of 1590. The primary purpose of the voyage was to raid Spanish treasure ships. Relieving the colonists was only a secondary objective.

It was now mid-August. White and the others had been at sea for five months. White knew the colonists must be wondering what had become of him. He tried not to think about the trouble that might have befallen them in his absence. His concerns had a very personal foundation. Among those he had left behind were his daughter Eleanor Dare, her husband Ananias, and their baby, Virginia, christened just days before White departed for England.

White couldn't help smiling at the thought of his precious granddaughter, the first European child born in the New World. She would soon celebrate her third birthday. How he longed to see her, to know that she was safe.

A gull cried harshly, startling White out of his reverie. The crew had begun making preparations to weigh anchor. As darkness descended, he gazed again at the shoreline. Clouds of smoke rose into the air above the distant trees. White studied the landmarks. The smoke seemed to come from the approximate location of Roanoke, where he had last seen the colonists. It could be a sign that the settlement was alive and well.

The next day he and several members of the crew rowed to the island. Trudging through the sand under a scorching August sun, White reassured himself. He had no doubt the colonists, a group of more than one hundred capable men and women, had found a way to survive. They probably received help from friends they had made among the native people. They certainly could have relied on Manteo, a Croatoan baptized into the Christian faith around the same time White's granddaughter was christened.

Still, relations among the people inhabiting the New World had not been perfect. Knowing that trouble might arise while he was in England, White had told the colonists to carve a message on a tree if they left Roanoke. If they left in distress, they were to carve a cross above the message.

White drew closer to the source of the smoke. With a sinking heart, he realized this was only a woods fire. There was no sign of human life or activity. Weary and footsore, the group returned to their ships, planning to head for Roanoke in the morning.

August 17 dawned fair, but strong winds from the northeast whipped the ocean into a churning broth. Passing over the bar into the harbor proved to be a perilous undertaking. Waves washed over the *Hopewell*'s deck. The *Moonlight* capsized, and seven crew members drowned.

By the time they were able to set out again, it was dark. They overshot Roanoke by a quarter mile. White's dismay was replaced by hope when he saw the light of a huge fire through the woods. This time it had to be Eleanor, Ananias, and the others.

At daybreak they went ashore. To White's disappointment, they found burning grass and trees instead of a signal fire. Through the woods they trekked, with White in the lead, his heart in his throat. Everything would be fine, he assured himself. Any minute now he would hear voices and the sounds of civilization. Little Virginia would run to meet him, arms outstretched.

He stopped. Directly before him stood a tree with three letters carved on it: C R O.

White told his companions about the instructions he had given the planters and pointed out that there was no cross above the letters to indicate distress. Continuing on, they arrived at the settlement.

The houses White had expected to see were gone. In their place was an open area enclosed by a fortlike barrier made of trees. White paused at the entrance and stared at one huge tree in particular. The bark had been removed. About five feet from the ground, eight letters were carved: C R O A T O A N.

Inside the enclosure, heavy items made of iron or lead were strewn about, almost covered by grass and weeds. Not far away White found several chests belonging to him. Someone had broken them open and dumped out the contents. Covers had been torn off books. Pictures and maps had been left on the ground to be ruined by the elements.

Still, to White's way of thinking, the message on the tree was one of hope. The planters must have gone to Croatoan Island, perhaps with Manteo.

Through the night the weather worsened. The sea rose up as if in anger, smashing in furious waves against the ships. Jagged bolts of lightning struck dangerously close. The next morning, as the crew of the *Hopewell* attempted to set sail for Croatoan, the anchor cable broke. They dropped a second anchor, which they also lost. They had one anchor left, and food was running low. White agreed with the captain that it would best to head for the West Indies, where they could obtain food and water and spend the winter. In the spring they could return to Croatoan.

But Mother Nature would not have it so. The *Hopewell* was blown out to sea in a violent storm. White reached Plymouth, England, on October 24, 1590. He never returned to Croatoan.

Although Sir Walter Raleigh and others continued to search for the Roanoke colonists off and on over the years, they were never found. Were they attacked by Spaniards? Were they among the victims slaughtered in 1605 by Powhatan's warriors? Did they intermarry with the Croatoans? Nobody knows for sure. The fate of the Lost Colony remains a mystery to this day.

Blackbeard's Demise
· 1718 ·

B ritish Navy Lieutenant Robert Maynard had no illusions about the extreme danger of his mission. As the two small warships under his command sailed up the James River toward the Atlantic Ocean, he knew he might never see the shores of Virginia again. His task required secrecy and stealth, courage, cleverness, and a willingness to die if necessary. He only hoped the ammunition and small arms he carried onboard would be sufficient.

The year was 1718. The month was November. Maynard and his crew of seaworthy souls were headed for Ocracoke Island off Cape Hatteras, North Carolina. The planters and settlers of the colony had appealed to Royal Governor Alexander Spotswood of Virginia for help in ridding their waters of a most unholy terror. In response, Spotswood had ordered Maynard and his men into action. Their assignment was to "beard the lion in his den." In this particular case, the quarry was a "sea" lion. And his beard was most fearsome and black.

The real name of the person they were after was Edward Teach, Edward Thatch, or, some say, Edward Drummond—but that matters little. The name the world remembers him by even now, nearly three hundred years later, is Blackbeard, and that name was real enough to anyone who sailed the high seas during the early years of the eighteenth century.

Born in 1680, Edward Teach was a native of England, probably Bristol or London. He came from a wealthy family and was well educated. Teach began his career as a privateer for England's Queen Anne during the War of the Spanish Succession.

Around 1713, he took up pirating full-time for his own amusement and profit. An apprentice to Captain Benjamin Hornigold, a notorious pirate of the times, Teach was an excellent student and soon created his own empire by preying on lightly armed merchant ships.

As Lieutenant Maynard gazed at the choppy, dark waters of the James River that November afternoon, he recalled one of Blackbeard's most recent foul deeds. In May of 1718, the devilish pirate had set up a blockade in the harbor of Charleston, South Carolina. Positioning his ships end to end across the bay, he held Charleston hostage for several weeks, demanding money, supplies, and medicine. It was the culmination of a reign of terror during which Blackbeard had acquired four vessels and more than three hundred henchmen.

To everyone's surprise, shortly after the blockade Blackbeard surrendered to North Carolina Governor Charles Eden. The dreaded pirate accepted a pardon and took an "oath of obedience." He even set up housekeeping with a wife (his thirteenth or fourteenth, no one was sure which) in the town of Bath. Within two years, however, he had resumed his murderous plundering with even greater zeal.

Maynard shook his head. If even half the stories about Blackbeard's cruelty and carnage were true, he would be doing the whole world a huge favor by cutting the rogue down. But he would have to be very careful. Edward Teach was no fool. He undoubtedly had spies everywhere. Maynard planned to stop any craft he met on the way—not only to confirm Blackbeard's whereabouts but also to prevent those onboard from going to warn the outlaw.

On November 21, about four days after he left Virginia, Maynard reached the mouth of Ocracoke Inlet. En route he had learned from passing schooners that Blackbeard's ship was indeed anchored at his favorite spot on the south side of the island. It was evening. The chilly breezes of late fall and the shadows of night swirled in the mist surrounding Maynard's boats. Even though the British commander had been extremely careful, he knew he could not count on the element of surprise. In fact, Blackbeard had already placed his ship in a posture of defense. He was clearly expecting company.

At dawn on November 22, Maynard ordered the attack. With a skilled seaman at the helm, the Royal Navy sloop bore down on the pirate's craft. Suddenly, with a sickening scraping sound, it ran aground in shallow water.

One can only imagine Blackbeard's glee as he blasted his stranded antagonist broadside with swan shot and scrap iron, instantly disabling twenty men. As the smoke cleared, an eerie silence descended over Ocracoke Inlet. The deck of Maynard's ship was empty, save for the wounded and the dead.

With a fiendish chuckle, Blackbeard signaled a dozen or so of his band to join him in boarding the crippled sloop. This was really too easy, he thought. No challenge at all.

In the hold below the decks of the British vessel, Lieutenant Maynard and the rest of his surviving crew members crouched in darkness. They listened as lifeboats hit the water with a splash. They heard men climbing up the sides of the ship. Loud thuds overhead told them the pirates had leaped over the gunwale.

"Now!" exclaimed Maynard. He rushed up on deck with his men and confronted a hellish sight. An enormous, muscular wildman towered over them, brandishing a cutlass in his huge right hand. Dressed in black from his boots to his broad-brimmed hat, he sported several pistols and knives in a wide leather belt, or bandolier, across his chest. He had twisted his long, coal-black hair and beard into "tails," tying them with colored cloth. Entwined in a few of the tails were slow-burning matches that sent forth smoke to billow around his ghastly face. The spark of madness in his eyes glinted off the two-foot knife clenched between his discolored teeth. He growled deep in his throat like a beast.

Maynard had never met the infamous Blackbeard, but he im- mediately recognized him. The sailors began a fierce, hand-to-hand battle against the buccaneers. Blade clanked against blade. Shots rang out, and the sea was soon tinctured blood red. Maynard and his men fired at Blackbeard, wounding him at least five times. Teach's body was gushing blood, yet the pirate still stood his ground. Cursing, he drew one of his spare pistols, cocked it—and fell down dead. All the pirates who had come aboard with their leader were either killed or taken prisoner.

At this point the second schooner under Maynard's command moved in to attack Blackbeard's vessel. The few remaining buccaneers surrendered, their eyes wide in fear and astonishment as they watched Maynard's men hang Blackbeard's severed head on the prow of the British ship. Later, many would swear the pirate king's headless body swam three times around the sloop before disappearing in a slow dive. From that moment on, the channel would be known as Teach's Hole.

Blackbeard's surviving crew members were tried, convicted, and hanged. In the course of the investigation, it was strongly implied by witnesses that North Carolina's genial Governor Eden and Chief Justice Tobias Knight had been protecting the pirate in exchange for a share of his illgotten booty. They were never convicted.

With the death of Blackbeard, the colonists along the Carolina coast breathed a sigh of relief and resumed their normal lives. The Golden Age of Piracy was over. Yet on a clear night, the natives of Ocracoke Island claim, Blackbeard's body swims slowly through the water, looking for its skull. Others swear the scoundrel's ghost prowls the beaches under the pale moonlight, in order to guard buried gold. No one ever found Blackbeard's treasure.

A Fight for Independence
·1771·

To Captain William "Black Bill" Alexander, one thing was certain: the wagons headed for Hillsborough with munitions for Governor Tryon's troops must be prevented from delivering their cargo. His view was heartily supported by the nine men who met with him secretly one evening in early May 1771 in what is now Cabarrus County, North Carolina.

The men had blackened their faces with gunpowder to avoid being identified. Their own family members would have trouble recognizing them, Captain Alexander noted with satisfaction. Even so, he was able to name each man. They were brothers James, William, and John White and their cousin William, born and raised on the banks of Rocky River; Robert Caruthers; Robert Davis; Benjamin Cockrane; James Ashmore; and Joshua Hadley.

All ten men, including Alexander, were members of pioneer families who had settled the western part of the Royal Colony of North Carolina. Their grievances with Royal Governor William Tryon and other officials from the colony's eastern section dated back many years. In fact, most residents of the frontier counties were fed up with the lack of representation in government, dishonest sheriffs, and illegal fees imposed by the ruling class. What they hated more than anything else was the fact that taxes were levied only on the poll, which meant rich and poor paid equal amounts.

At the heart of the conflict were the essential social and economic differences between the eastern and western sections of the colony. In *The War of the Regulation and the Battle of Alamance, May 16, 1771*, William S. Powell writes:

> In the East, the people were almost entirely of English descent. It was here that an aristocratic form of society prevailed, based upon large plantations and slave labor. . . . In the West, Scotch-Irish and German ancestries were predominant. Here plantations were small and slaves were few in number. For the most part, the West was still in the pioneer stage. The forms and ideals of society were democratic. . . . Between the two sections stretched a sparsely settled region of pine forest which formed a natural barrier between them.

Over the years, attempts to reason with officials had been ignored or met with harsh reprisals. In 1768, determined to "regulate" their own affairs, disgruntled frontiersmen banded together, calling themselves Regulators. Wealthy eastern North Carolinians referred to them as "a mob."

Thus it was that two years before the Boston Tea Party, four years before shots were fired at Lexington and Concord, and five years before America declared its independence from England, the people of North Carolina's "backcountry" staged their own revolution against British rule. Violence, lawlessness, and terrorism reigned as Regulators rioted in the streets and brutally attacked figures of authority, many of them innocent of any wrongdoing.

"Black Bill" Alexander and his group would have preferred to settle their differences with the British government peacefully. However, by 1771 they no longer believed that was possible. Unless they took action, the gunpowder and flints being transported to Hillsborough that very night would be used against the Regulators. The lives of friends, neighbors, and family members were at stake.

Standing in a circle, the men swore a solemn oath not to reveal their mission to anyone. Although most of them were able to start the journey on horseback, the White brothers straggled behind on foot. Their father had taken the family's two horses with him on an errand. In *Sketches of Western North Carolina*, C. L. Hunter reports:

> Fortunately for their feet, they met their father returning home with his burdens, and immediately demanded the use of his horses. The gentleman, not knowing who they were (as black as Satan himself) pleaded heartily for the horses until he could carry home his bags of meal; but his petitions were in vain. The boys (his sons) ordered him to dismount, removed the bags from the horses, and placed them by the side of the road.

Mounted at last, the White brothers joined their comrades. At Phifer's Hill, just a few miles west of what is now Concord, North Carolina, the group came upon the governor's convoy of munitions wagons. Again according to Hunter:

> They immediately unloaded the wagons, stove in the heads of the kegs, threw the powder into a pile, tore the blankets into strips, made a train of powder a considerable distance from the pile, and then Major James White fired a pistol into the train, which produced a tremendous explosion. A stave from the pile struck White on the forehead, and cut him severely.

Captain Alexander and company, known from that day forward as the Cabarrus Black Boys, succeeded in their mission. However, the larger effort of the Regulators failed. On May 16, 1771, Governor Tryon's troops, consisting of about 1,300 highly trained, well-equipped militiamen, crushed 2,500 Regulators at Alamance Creek. Unorganized and lacking adequate leadership, the Regulators did not even have enough firepower to defend themselves.

Accounts of the two-hour Battle of Alamance Creek vary. Some say each side lost nine men; others say the dead included nine Royalists and twenty Regulators. Other sources number the total casualties at almost three hundred. Fifteen Regulators were taken prisoner, and one was executed the next day. Six more were hanged and the rest pardoned.

In the months that followed, thousands of Regulators turned themselves in to receive a pardon from the royal governor. Among them were James Ashmore and Joshua Hadley, who divulged the names of the other Cabarrus Black Boys in order to save their own skins. In response, Colonel Moses Alexander, a magistrate under the colonial government, reportedly remarked, "By virtue of the Governor's proclamation, you are pardoned, but you are the first that ought to be hanged." Their identity revealed, the rest of the Black Boys fled to Georgia, where they remained in hiding for four years.

In April of 1775, a much larger rebellion was ignited when British troops skirmished with seventy minutemen at Lexington, Massachusetts. Historian William S. Powell writes:

> The real significance of the Regulators' struggle and the Battle of Alamance lies in the fact that it stood as a grand object lesson to the people of the whole country. It set them to thinking of armed resistance and showed them how weak might be the British effort to suppress a full-scale revolution. The North Carolina troops, at least, were able to appreciate the feelings of such an army.

And what became of the Cabarrus Black Boys? William Edward Fitch tells us in *Some Neglected History of North Carolina*: "When the drama of the Revolution opened, these same 'Black Boys' stood up manfully for the cause of American freedom, and nobly assisted in achieving, on many a hard-fought battle-field, the independence of our country."

Brother Against Brother
· 1780 ·

On June 19, 1780, about thirty men from Lincoln County, North Carolina, responded to a call for help from their friend and neighbor Adam Reep. Following his instructions, they met him at midnight at Ramsey's Ford, muskets in hand. One by one they presented their guns to him for inspection. All were in good order except for the shattered musket belonging to a young lad in the group. Reep told the boy he would get a better weapon for him when Colonel Locke and the rest of the Whig forces arrived.

More than four years had passed since troops loyal to King George of England had killed eight Whigs—also called Patriots—in a skirmish at Lexington, Massachusetts, igniting a full-scale revolution against the Crown. Since then, many battles had been waged in America's northern colonies. Prior to 1778, fighting in the South had been limited. The British—also called Tories—had been turned back at Moore's Creek Bridge, North Carolina, in February of 1776. Patriots had successfully defended Fort Sullivan, South Carolina, in June of that same year.

Near the end of 1778, the war in the South expanded when a British seaborne expedition of 3,500 men captured Savannah, Georgia. Three years later, at the battle of Guilford Court House in North Carolina, Major General Nathanael Greene's troops would force the British to retreat, effectively ending British control in the Carolinas and paving the way for their ultimate downfall at Yorktown, Virginia.

In June of 1780, however, Lincoln County patriots still had much to gain—and lose—by taking a stand against the king. Recent British triumphs at Charleston and Waxhaws, South Carolina, did not bode well. It was clear that Lord Cornwallis, the British commander, intended to advance into North Carolina at his earliest convenience.

In fact, the Tories had already begun to gather in Lincoln County under the direction of British sympathizers Lieutenant Colonel John Moore and Major Nicholas Welch. William L. Carpenter described the situation in an article for *Lincoln County Heritage:*

> Moore's exact intentions are unknown, but it is assumed that he intended to rid the country of the small bands of Patriots operating in the area and/or to move against Patriot forces under the command of Gen. Griffith Rutherford camped near Charlotte. Rutherford was in charge of the militia in western North Carolina. On June 14 he received word that the Tories were assembling in Lincoln County. He issued orders to Col. Francis Locke of Rowan County and several other officers to raise men to disperse the Tories. On June 19 they assembled with 400 men on Mountain Creek, 16 miles east of Ramsour's Mill.

Shortly after daylight, Colonel Locke and a force of between five and six hundred Patriots joined Adam Reep. Although Reep was not a military officer, he was an accomplished scout, respected and trusted by Locke. Reep had already checked out the enemy's exact location, position, and numbers. He reported that the Loyalists outnumbered the Patriots nearly two to one.

Many years later Lincoln County native Wallace M. Reinhardt spoke at length with Adam Reep, by then far advanced in age. Based on Reep's recollections, Reinhardt described the scene that morning of June 20, 1780:

Reep's men mingling among Locke's troops were repeatedly asked if the Tories were brave enough to fight well; the answer from all was, "They will fight." Colonel Locke told Reep that as he was so well posted as to the grounds and positions of the enemy he should command his thirty men and use or move them as he like—"For I know you are an experienced scout." This was a great compliment and, as Reep said afterwards, almost brought tears from him.

At the first light of dawn, under cover of dense fog, Adam Reep guided the Whig forces through bushes and thickets to within half a mile of the British camp. Locke halted the troops and, according to Reinhardt's notes from his conversations with Reep, gave the following orders:

Captain Falls will continue on this road, as it runs across the hill to the Mill, and move up to within three or four hundred yards of the enemy (who were on top of the hill), halt, and wait until the main body is near enough to commence the attack from the south side. Captain Dobson will march over towards the creek and into Green's road (a road laid off by an English surveyor of that name) and will attack the enemy from that direction. Not a gun is to be fired until all are ready; the attack must be simultaneous.

Near the top of the hill stood a few oak trees, which offered some protection against sharpshooters. Eyewitnesses later reported that because of the heavy fog, the combatants could not see each other until they met at close range. And meet they did— one-on-one, hand-to-hand, on the hill. The fighting was intense, and as the fog lifted, the horrific scene was clearly revealed: neighbors, even brothers, clubbing each other with guns, shooting each other where they stood.

Reinhardt described Reep's recollections concerning Tory commander Nicholas Warlick, a native of Pennsylvania:

> Captain Warlick . . . ordered his roan horse . . . and mounting, he rode along the lines like a madman talking to his men and cheering them. "Never let it be said in after years we were whipped by a handful of Whigs."

As Warlick passed near the edge of the woods, a Patriot sharpshooter took aim. "The fine roan charger, much fretted and covered with foam and sweat, reared up and Captain Warlick tumbled off, dead," Reinhardt wrote.

By the time General Griffith Rutherford (who was a good man and a brave officer but never moved in a hurry, according to Reinhardt's report) arrived with Patriot reinforcements around noon, the battle was over. Records show that about one hundred men were killed at the Battle of Ramsour's Mill. Colonel Moore and about four hundred Tories made their escape after raising a false flag of truce. According to Reinhardt:

> The scene upon the battlefield was indescribable— dead men here and there, broken skulls, a few were seen with gun-locks sunk into their heads; disabled men moving about seeking help, men with shattered shoulders, broken arms and legs, while others were breathing their last breath. Shortly after the battle many women, children and old men came hunting for their loved ones.

Although historians often describe the American Civil War as a conflict that pitted brother against brother, the fight for independence eighty years earlier divided families with an equally sharp blade.

Today, a school playground graces the hill where Whigs and Tories once met in battle, where neighbor fought neighbor to the death. Swings, slides, and sandboxes surround a rectangular monument about four feet wide, five feet high, and two and one-half feet deep. It reads:

IN MEMORY OF NICHOLAS WARLICK, A LOYAL SUBJECT OF THE KING AND CAPTAIN OF VOLUN-TEERS WHO WITH HIS BROTHER PHILLIP WARLICK AND ISAREL [sic] SAIN DIED IN THE BATTLE OF RAMSOUR'S MILL HERE AND WERE BURIED IN ONE GRAVE JUNE 20, 1780.

Nearby, a low, granite boundary surrounds a mass grave that is the final resting place of soldiers from both sides whose bodies were not claimed by family or friends. Oak trees towering over the site are the only remaining witnesses to the slaughter.

Although the Battle of Ramsour's Mill usually does not make the "short list" of significant military encounters on American soil, some historians consider it a major turning point in the Revolutionary War. In general, prior to June 20, 1781, the war in the South was going against the Patriots. Success at Ramsour's Mill stemmed the tide of British aggression and laid the groundwork for a Patriot victory four months later at King's Mountain. From that point on, the struggle for American independence quickly gained momentum, ultimately resulting in a British surrender at Yorktown.

A Golden Opportunity
· 1799 ·

Like many twelve-year-old boys, Conrad Reed loved to hunt. He often took his bow and arrow to Meadow Creek near his home in what is now Cabarrus County, North Carolina. There he tried to perfect his aim by shooting at fish. The most he ever expected to gain from his efforts was a meal for his family. Occasionally he brought home an interesting rock or crawling creature that caught his eye.

On one particular fishing trip in the spring of 1799, Conrad picked up an object that would have an enormous effect on not only his life but also the history of the entire state.

Originally inhabited by Native American tribes, the area now known as Cabarrus County became home to a mixture of German and Scotch-Irish immigrants in the early 1740s. They settled among the gently rolling slate hills where game was plentiful and the red clay yielded a healthy crop of wheat, corn, and oats.

Conrad Reed's father was Johannes Ried, Riedt, or Rieth, a native of Germany whose name was anglicized to "John Reed." Reed was one of several thousand Hessians hired by Britain to fight the colonists during the American Revolution. In 1780, Reed and a group of his fellow mercenaries deserted King George III at the Battle of Camden, South Carolina. They made their way to the St. John's Lutheran Church Community, an area of North Carolina settled by Germans more than thirty years earlier.

Around 1784, Reed married Sarah Kaiser. As the years passed, the couple had several children. Early in 1799, Reed purchased 330 acres from the state of North Carolina, intending to use it as farmland to support his family. The property was located on Meadow Creek, a branch of the Rocky River.

Legend has it that one Sunday morning in early spring 1799, John and Sarah Reed went to church, leaving Conrad and his two sisters at home. In his book *North Carolina Picadillo*, John K. Rouse describes what happened next.

> While his father and mother were at church, Conrad decided to take his sisters to Meadow Creek to shoot fish with his bow and arrow. As they walked along the meandering creek, Conrad saw a bright yellow object shining in the sparkling water. He waded into the stream, picked up the curious looking stone about the size of a smoothing iron and carried it home. When John Reed returned home from church in late afternoon, Conrad showed his father the bright yellow stone that he had found in the creek.

The strange, wedge-shaped rock weighed about seventeen pounds. John Reed took it to nearby Concord, North Carolina, and showed it to his friend, silversmith William Atkinson. Atkinson could not identify it. Unconcerned, Reed carried the hunk of ore home and put it to work as a doorstop.

Three years passed with Conrad's peculiar stone serving admirably in its assigned role. According to William S. Powell in *North Carolina Through Four Centuries*, "In 1802 the elder Reed took the rock to Fayetteville where a jeweler fluxed the gold and ran it into a bar about six inches long. Not knowing its value, Reed accepted the $3.50 that he was offered for it."

In his book *Golden Promise in the Piedmont: The Story of John Reed's Mine*, Dr. Richard F. Knapp reports:

The merchant, whose name is now unknown, gladly paid him and received roughly $3,600 worth of gold. It was not long before Reed discovered his errors and supposedly recovered about a thousand dollars from the jeweler.

Within a year, Reed found more nuggets, some weighing up to twenty-eight pounds. More than forty years before gold fever broke out in California, hopeful prospectors streamed into Cabarrus County, North Carolina. Using every pick, shovel, and pan at their disposal, they joined in the search for the precious metal. According to Rouse, a man named Christian Ludwig Benzien of Salem at Wachovia wrote the following to friends in Germany:

> Probably the news has not yet reached Germany that for several months gold has been mined in Cabarrus County, North Carolina, about seventy miles southwest of here (the first in the United States). I have myself seen a piece of which was sent to me by Br. Jacob Loesch in Bethania to be smelted and it was very rich.

Before long a number of gold mining companies opened in North Carolina, employing an estimated thirty thousand workers from all over the world. Mines were established not only in Cabarrus but in Anson, Mecklenburg, Montgomery, and other counties. A mint was opened in Charlotte in 1838. Between 1800 and 1860, the population of the state more than doubled.

In his book *Golden Promise in the Piedmont*, Richard E. Knapp states, "All of the native gold coined by the federal mint before 1828 came from the Old North State, and gold mining at one point reputedly was second only to agriculture as an occupation in the state."

North Carolina led the nation in gold production until 1848. By then the veins had begun to run out. Deep mining was expensive and dangerous. Word traveled across the land that gold had been discovered at Sutter's Mill at the junction of the American and Sacramento rivers in California. Prospectors packed their gear, and the California gold rush was on. Gold mining continued in North Carolina well into the 1850s but gold became hard to get by the time the Civil War began.

Today, the streams and creeks of Cabarrus County still yield their share of bass, bream, catfish, and carp. Nevertheless, it would be fairly safe to bet that no Cabarrus County fisherman ever landed as fine a "catch" as young Conrad Reed.

The Story of Tsali
· 1838 ·

They stood side by side: the old man, his two sons, and his brother—four members of a tribe the white settlers called "Cherokee." It was spring in the Appalachian Mountains. The songs of the redbird and chickadee danced among the fragrant dogwood blossoms. The hills were cloaked in brilliant purple, pink, yellow, and green. But for these four men, the season held no joy. Eyes forward, expressions grim, they stared stoically into the face of death.

The year was 1838. Almost three hundred years had passed since Spanish explorer Hernando DeSoto had made his way into the mountains of Carolina and Georgia. There he discovered a tribe his chroniclers called "Chalaque," a name that later evolved into "Cherokee." The tribe called itself "Yunwiya" or "Ani-Yunwiya," meaning "real people" or "principal people."

During the years that followed DeSoto's visit, the Cherokees continually fought other tribes as well as the Europeans who arrived on DeSoto's heels. Indians, as the whites called America's native people, often survived the gun and hatchet only to succumb to the ravages of smallpox or rum. Hatred rose and fell in a bloody tide, sending waves of destruction and death across the land.

By 1761, Cherokee warriors, once estimated at 5,000, numbered only 2,300. During the American Revolution, their population declined further as they fought on the side of the British. In spite of these hardships, by 1828 the "principal people" were among the most civilized of all native tribes. They had a written language, laws, a newspaper, and their own supreme court, constitution, and capital city.

Unfortunately, these achievements did not save them from further injury. In 1836, over the opposition of Cherokee chief John Ross and nearly sixteen thousand of his tribe, the United States Senate ratified a treaty signed by just a few hundred Cherokee tribesmen. Under that agreement—the Treaty of New Echota— the Cherokee nation ceded to the United States all its remaining territory east of the Mississippi. In exchange, the eastern Cherokees received five million dollars and a joint interest in territory already occupied by the western Cherokees, as well as a small tract in what is now Kansas.

Following ratification of the treaty, only about two thousand Indians left the area voluntarily. President Andrew Jackson placed General Winfield Scott in command of seven thousand soldiers and ordered him to remove the remaining Cherokees by force. James Mooney described the scene in *History, Myths, and Sacred Formulas of the Cherokees:*

> Families at dinner were startled by the sudden gleam of bayonets in the doorway and rose up to be driven with blows and oaths along the weary miles of trail that led to the stockade. Men were seized in their fields or going along the road, women were taken from their wheels and children from their play. In many cases, on turning for one last look as they crossed the ridge, they saw their homes in flames, fired by the lawless rabble that followed on the heels of the soldiers to loot and pillage.

One mild spring day in May of 1838, an old man named Tsali (called "Charley" by whites) learned that several United States Army soldiers were on their way to his cabin, high in the hills.

Tsali had heard all about the Treaty of New Echota, including the fact that President Jackson had rejected a suggestion that a limited number of Cherokees be allowed to remain in the mountains. To Tsali and his tribe, Jackson's conduct was inexcusable. He seemed to have forgotten that in 1814, Cherokee allies had saved his life at the Battle of Horseshoe Bend.

Tsali knew hundreds of his people had already escaped the Army and fled, hiding themselves in remote mountain caves. He had hoped Scott's troops would overlook his cabin, but when he heard they were coming, he devised a plan. Instead of confronting the soldiers when they arrived, Tsali and his family pretended to submit meekly.

The soldiers seized old Tsali along with his wife, his three sons and their families, and his brother. Although the Indians appeared submissive, the women had concealed knives and tomahawks in their clothing. As they walked to the stockade, they slipped the weapons to the men, who awaited further instructions from Tsali.

Trudging through the woods along a trail that led to the stockade, the captives sometimes stumbled over thick tree roots and sharp rock edges. Tsali's wife found the journey especially difficult. Advanced in years, she could not walk as quickly as the others. A soldier, irritated by her slow pace, prodded her with his bayonet.

Tsali's anger flared. His patience with the white invaders had reached its limit. Quietly but firmly, he spoke in Cherokee to his family, knowing their captors could not understand what he was saying. Suddenly, on his command, the Indians attacked. The soldiers cried out in surprise as their guns were wrenched from their hands.

Accounts of the incident vary. Some claim a gun went off by accident, killing one soldier. Others report that two soldiers were killed immediately and three were mortally wounded. In any case, Tsali and his family fled into the mountains, where they joined a group of their kinsmen high up on what is now Clingman's Dome. The Indians there were surviving as best they could, eating roots and wild berries. Their only hope was that General Scott would eventually give up searching.

Indeed, Scott had already realized that it was impractical to track down all the fugitives. When he heard what "old Charley" had done, he came up with a proposal. According to James Mooney:

> General Scott finally tendered them a proposition through (Colonel) W. H. Thomas, their most trusted friend, that if they would surrender Charley and his party for punishment, the rest would be allowed to remain until their case could be adjusted by the government.

William Holland Thomas had long ago earned the affection and respect of the Cherokees. As a child he was adopted by Chief Yonaguska, who gave him the nickname "Will-Usdi" or "Little Will." Although the Cherokees suffered many broken treaties and hollow promises in their dealings with white settlers, Will-Usdi retained their trust. Scott knew they would seriously consider any message delivered by such a dear friend.

Refusing Scott's offer of a military escort, Thomas set out alone. According to Mooney, he found Tsali's hiding place and, with a heavy heart, presented the general's proposal. In response, the old man, his two oldest sons, and his brother made their way slowly down the mountainside. Mooney described what awaited them below.

> By command of General Scott, Charley, his brother, and the two elder sons were shot near the mouth of Tuckasegee, a detachment of Cherokee prisoners being compelled to do the shooting in order to impress upon the Indians the fact of their utter helplessness.

In October of 1838, about thirteen thousand captives started the long march through Tennessee, Kentucky, Illinois, Missouri, and Arkansas into Indian Territory west of the Mississippi. Along the way, an estimated four thousand people died from hunger, exposure, and disease as they walked what later became known as the "Trail of Tears."

Nearly a year after the march began, refugees were still scattered throughout the mountains of North Carolina and Tennessee. Eventually, thanks to additional efforts by William Thomas, they received permission from the government to stay. From those fugitives originated the present eastern band of Cherokee.

When today's "principal people" recall this painful episode in their history, they think not only of the hardships and hunger, the death and despair, they also recall the story of old Tsali, his two sons, and his brother—four courageous members of their tribe who sacrificed themselves so that more than a thousand Cherokees could remain in the coves and hollows of the Blue Ridge.

The Highest Peak in the East
· 1857 ·

Elisha Mitchell paused for a moment on his journey upward and gazed across the peaks and valleys of western North Carolina's Black Mountains. In his younger days he'd had more than enough energy for the climb, thrashing through dense laurel thickets and tangling with snakes and bears. Now in his early sixties, the educator, minister, and scientist found such a hike less than appealing. As far as he was concerned, he had accomplished his goal on previous trips; nevertheless, it appeared he would have to make one last climb to prove his claim incontestably.

All around him rhododendron and mountain laurel bloomed in a riotous symphony of white, purple, and pink, their deep green leaves striking a cool accent note. It was a land of rare beauty and stark contrasts, of jagged rocks and delicate blossoms, gurgling streams and screeching panthers, of roots securing themselves deep in the earth and trees reaching for the clouds with their fingertips.

The date was June 27, 1857—a Saturday. That afternoon, Dr. Mitchell, who had received an honorary doctor of divinity degree in 1840, had bid farewell to his eighteen-year-old son, Charles, and started hiking. He was headed to the upper Cane River valley about ten miles away, where he intended to confer with "Big Tom" Wilson and other guides who had accompanied him on his trips into the mountains over the past twenty-two years. Although somewhat advanced in age, Mitchell was a large, vigorous man and an experienced climber, familiar with the terrain. He told Charles he would see him on Monday at the mountain lodge.

Elisha Mitchell first encountered the long range of peaks and ridges known as the Black Mountains in the late 1820s while conducting the North Carolina Geological Survey. A native of Connecticut, he graduated from Yale in 1818 with a master of arts degree. He initially became a mathematics and natural philosophy instructor at the University of North Carolina at Chapel Hill and later taught chemistry, geology, and mineralogy.

In 1827 he made his first trip to the Black Mountains about thirty miles northeast of Asheville. At that time Grandfather Mountain was thought to be the highest point in the region. However, to Mitchell's eye, "the Blacks," as the Black Mountains were often called, appeared higher. He decided more study was needed.

During the summer of 1835, he came back to the region. Using barometric pressure readings and a complex mathematical formula, he estimated the heights of several mountains. On that visit he climbed what he later described as "the highest peak of the Black." According to his calculations, its elevation was 6,476 feet above sea level.

As it turned out, Elisha Mitchell had made a discovery of national importance. At the time, New Hampshire's Mt. Washington, measuring 6,288 feet above sea level, was believed to be the highest peak in eastern America. Mitchell's readings showed that the North Carolina mountain was almost two hundred feet taller.

In 1838 Elisha Mitchell returned again to western North Carolina. In his mind there was still a chance that another peak in the Blacks might be taller than the one he had measured three years earlier. He and a guide ascended the southern end of the range to a complex of three peaks. Barometric readings indicated that one of the peaks was 6,581 feet above sea level, about one hundred feet higher than the peak Mitchell had measured in 1835.

Back in Chapel Hill, uncertainties plagued Mitchell. Had he really found the highest peak in the Black Mountains? In an effort to remove all doubt, he returned to the mountains in the summer of 1844, even though he did not relish scaling the heights again. The day before the climb he wrote, "To morrow I am expecting to ascend the Black Mountain I hope for the last time. I shall probably now reach the highest summit."

Accompanied by two guides, Dr. Mitchell clambered up the slopes. Just a month shy of his fifty-first birthday, he found the trek to be an uphill battle in every sense. In a letter to his wife, Mary, he called it a "dreadful journey."

Using a new mountain barometer, Mitchell took readings on the three peaks he had visited in 1838. This time he calculated the pinnacle to be more than 6,600 feet above sea level. It seemed clear to him that this must be the "top of the Blacks." Another letter from Mitchell to his wife described the hazardous descent: "Jumped along the rocks down the bed of the river, got some dreadful falls and soused in till it was dark—a heavy rain which further aided in wetting me through and through. . . ."

In September of 1855, Thomas Lanier Clingman, a U.S. congressman from North Carolina, made an excursion to the Blacks. Clingman had been one of Dr. Mitchell's students at the University of North Carolina at Chapel Hill. Since Mitchell seemed unsure about his discovery, Clingman decided to take some measurements of his own. He reported his findings in a lengthy article published in the *Washington City Spectator*. In that article he stated that Mitchell had not reached the highest portion of the Black Mountain range but that he, Clingman, had.

The controversy between Clingman and Mitchell grew into a serious feud, eroding the friendship the two men had established at Chapel Hill. Mitchell did not dispute the fact that the peak described by Clingman was the highest, but he insisted it was the same peak he had ascended and measured in 1838 and 1844. Unfortunately, his accounts of those two trips did not match Clingman's description of the route and natural features leading to the highest peak. Therefore, Clingman pointed out, Mitchell could not be talking about the same mountain.

On June 27, 1857, Elisha Mitchell stood alone on the steep slopes, determined to validate his claim. In his pack he carried only a few basic items, including the mathematical instruments he would need. That morning, he had written to Mary:

> We are here two thirds of the way from the base of the mountain to the top. Charles and myself with William [a servant boy] keeping bachelor's hall, getting on very well—in excellent health—living mostly on corn bread and bacon.

Mary never saw or heard from her husband again. When Dr. Mitchell failed to meet his son on Monday, family and friends became worried, even though they knew there were several possible explanations for his delay. Thursday morning Charles headed into the Cane River valley. Upon arriving at Big Tom Wilson's house, he learned his father had never shown up there.

By sundown on Friday, a group of about eighteen mountaineers were on their way up the mountain in search of Mitchell. Other search parties were also formed but not until Tuesday, July 7, did the searchers have any luck. About a quarter mile west of the highest peak of the Blacks, a group led by Big Tom Wilson came across an impression in the moss. A short distance away the broken trunk of a small balsam bore a footprint. Another impression on the root of a balsam convinced Big Tom that they were on the professor's trail. He was right.

In *A History of Mt. Mitchell and the Black Mountains*, S. Kent Schwarzkopf wrote:

> On following the creek for a short distance, Big Tom apprised his fellow searchers of his belief that they might find Mitchell at the base of a waterfall just ahead. In the following passage, Big Tom related what happened on his reaching the top of the falls:

"I walked out on the log and saw his [Mitchell's] hat and called to the boys. . . ."

Mitchell himself was located several feet below the surface of a fifteen-foot-deep pool, tangled in a rhododendron snag. His watch had stopped at 8:19 P.M.

Dr. Mitchell's supporters continued to defend his claim after his death, contending that he had reached the high peak of the range in 1835 but simply underestimated its height. Mitchell's guide substantiated this assertion when he described the route taken on the 1835 climb. Mitchell apparently had been confused when he insisted that the mountain he ascended and measured in 1838 and 1844 was the mountain measured by Clingman; in truth, Clingman measured the peak Mitchell had measured in 1835. Clingman did not challenge the final pro-Mitchell article, published in March 1858.

Although originally buried in Asheville, Dr. Mitchell's body was later moved to the top of the mountain he first called "the highest peak of the Black"—a mountain that now bears his name. Mt. Mitchell's true elevation is 6,684 feet above sea level. Toward the end of the century, the second highest point in the range was given the name Clingman's Peak.

The War in the Mountains
· 1862 ·

In the spring of 1862, L. McKesson "Keith" Blalock of Watauga County, North Carolina, enlisted in the Confederate Army. This was not unusual for a young man from the mountains. The Old North State provided between one-sixth and one-seventh of all Confederate troops during the War Between the States. So many volunteered in the early days of the war that they could not be properly equipped.

What was a bit unusual about Keith Blalock's desire for a gray uniform was the fact that he was a Unionist—one of a fair number of North Carolinians who opposed secession and sympathized with the position of the federal government.

In the beginning, most of the state's residents had been either against seceding from the union or uncommitted. However, in April of 1861, sentiment changed dramatically. Confederate forces took command of Fort Sumter in the harbor of Charleston, South Carolina, and President Abraham Lincoln called on all loyal states to supply soldiers to crush the rebellion.

The earth must have shaken as citizens of Tennessee, Virginia, Arkansas, and North Carolina jumped off the fence they were sitting on. All four states cast their lot with the Confederacy, yet, like many other areas of the South, the mountains of western North Carolina still harbored quite a few Union sympathizers.

Keith Blalock's motive for joining the rebel troops was simple. A healthy fellow in his midtwenties, he could not avoid being drafted into the army. His plan, therefore, was to enlist. At the first opportunity, ideally during a battle, he planned to slip across the lines to join the Yankees. That way he would be listed as "missing" instead of being labeled a deserter or traitor whose family would be fair game for violent anti-Unionists.

In March 1862, when Keith arrived in Kinston, North Carolina, to join the 26th Regiment, he was not alone. His companion, he told the other soldiers, was his kid brother, Sam, age sixteen. Sam was short and slight of build, weighing only about 130 pounds, but he seemed to be a tough, determined lad, fond of adventure, and not one to shirk his duties. Assigned the position of "Mess Wife," Sam prepared rations and packed camp equipment for transport. He shared Keith's tent. No one remarked on the fact that Sam never joined the other men in the swimming hole.

One week went by and then another. To Keith's dismay, the regiment remained garrisoned in Kinston, far from Yankee lines. Of course, he could always hike a hundred miles into Virginia on the slim chance that he would survive and avoid capture. He could also try to swim the Albemarle Sound. However, in addition to being dangerous, even foolhardy, choosing either option would brand him as a deserter. Besides, he had to think about Sam, who depended on him for protection. Somehow, together, they had to gracefully exit the Long Gray Line.

Before too long, a solution came to Keith Blalock. After shedding his clothes, he took a deep breath and plunged into a thicket of poison oak, coating his body thoroughly. Not surprisingly, he broke out in a horrendous rash. The medic who examined him feared a contagious disease and declared him unfit for service. He was discharged.

Sam Blalock was also discharged. He did not have a rash, and he was not sent home because he was young and somewhat frail. No, Keith Blalock's kid brother was relieved of duty as soon as commander Zebulon B. Vance was told the truth: Sam was not a sixteen-year-old boy. She was a twenty-year-old woman—Keith's wife, Malinda Pritchard Blalock.

In one roster of North Carolina's Civil War troops Malinda is listed as "Mrs. L. M. Blalock." Beside her name is the notation: "Discharged for being a woman."

The incident caused quite a stir, but the Blalocks' adventures were just beginning. Even though Keith had been officially and properly discharged, Confederate draft officers near his home noticed that he recovered from his "disease" rather quickly. They decided he was fit to return to duty.

Informed that he could either reenlist or be harshly penalized under the new draft law, Keith once again took drastic action. This time he and Malinda headed for the hills, disappearing into the thick forests on Grandfather Mountain. Soon they were joined by others who refused to serve the Southern cause, for whatever reason.

The authorities hunted them down, but Keith and his band opened fire. Wounded, Keith scrambled farther up the mountain and hid until the recruiters gave up searching. He and Malinda then fled to Tennessee. There they joined one of the most dreaded and ruthless Unionists of them all, Colonel George W. Kirk.

Kirk's regiments were under direct orders from General John M. Schofield, Department of the Ohio. Armed with Spencer repeating rifles and often mounted on stolen horses, his Second and Third Regiment of North Carolina Mounted Infantry—or "Home Yankees" as they were called—waged a private, personal war against mountaineers whose sympathies lay with the Confederacy.

Keith and Malinda Blalock's participation in Kirk's campaigns led author William R. Trotter to nickname them "the Bonnie and Clyde of Watauga County." During one battle with their former neighbors, Malinda was shot in the shoulder. In another encounter, a man Keith had wounded held his ground long enough to shoot out one of Keith's eyes.

When it came to guerrilla warfare in the mountains, nothing was sacred and no one was safe. Each attack prompted revenge, and revenge prompted further attacks. In February of 1865, a

Confederate mob stormed into Coffey Gap, looking for Austin Coffey, a Union sympathizer. Coffey was not home, but a neighbor, James Boyd, told the mob where he could be found. Austin Coffey was taken away and killed in cold blood.

In his book *Bushwhackers! The Civil War in North Carolina*, William R. Trotter states:

> Acre for acre, there was probably more gunfighting and gratuitous cold-blooded murder in Appalachian North Carolina during the Civil War than there was in any comparable chunk of the Wild West during any four-year period you care to name.

With Robert E. Lee's surrender at Appomattox in April of 1865, the Blalocks' military careers were officially over, but Keith's thirst for revenge had not been fully slaked. Austin Coffey was his stepfather, and Keith had a score to settle with James Boyd.

In February 1866, nearly a year after the end of the war, Blalock shot Boyd with a rifle at close range, killing him instantly. He was arrested but later pardoned by Governor William W. Holden, a Union sympathizer.

In their later years, the Blalocks took up farming in Mitchell County. Keith ran for the state legislature in 1874 but was defeated. Around 1892, he and Malinda moved to Texas but later returned to North Carolina. At least four children were born to the couple.

Malinda died a natural death in 1901. Twelve years later, Keith was operating a hand car on a mountain railroad when it missed a curve on a steep grade. The car plunged off the track, and Keith was killed.

Scarcity and
Speculation
· 1863 ·

By the spring of 1863, the conflict known variously as The Civil War, The War Between the States, and The War For States' Rights had reached middle age. Its participants had lost much of the enthusiasm they exhibited in the younger years of the conflict, but they were not yet willing to concede that their differences should be laid to rest. A "midlife crisis" was inevitable.

It was during this stage of the war that a group of women in Salisbury, North Carolina, reached their boiling point. They decided to take the law into their own hands to right what they saw as a grievous wrong.

As wives and mothers of Confederate soldiers, the women of Salisbury were no strangers to sacrifice. When North Carolina seceded from the Union in May 1861, they had gritted their teeth and plunged bravely into a bleak new world—one that tried their patience, wore out their bodies, and wearied their souls. They supported the cause that had taken their men away, leaving them to struggle with every aspect of daily life. However, they had a big problem with a certain group of people: those who practiced speculation.

In one sense, speculation—the purchase and sale of goods, land, or anything else, with the expectation of deriving profit from fluctuations in price—could be viewed as a shrewd business move. Speculators were highly skilled at stockpiling scarce items and selling them out of state at prices the average local citizen couldn't possibly pay. Among the papers of Governor Zebulon B. Vance are many letters describing the situation. One reads:

> The leather is put up in lots of 250 sides and sold to speculators at $4.00 and $4.50 per pound! Your correspondent went himself in person . . . and though he laid his case before them, that he had 6 little barefoot children that must have shoes, and offered to give any reasonable price for leather—just one side. But the reply was, if we sell to one man privately we must sell to others, and we will not do it. In the name of the Great God of the universe, what are we to do?

The children of Salisbury were not only barefoot but starving. Many families had not tasted meat for weeks, even months. Those who did not already have gardens could not even raise their own vegetables. Basic food items—potatoes, peas, and beans, for example—were either too scarce or too expensive for the average person to obtain. In a 1983 article for *The State*, Tom F. Skipper noted that meat sold for up to $140 per pound, flour for $50 a barrel, and chickens for $300 per dozen.

Similar conditions prevailed throughout the state. An unsigned letter to Governor Vance in February of 1863 revealed desperate circumstances in Bladen County: "We the common people has to hav bread or blood & we are bound boath men & women to hav it or die in the attempt . . . it seems that all harts is turned to gizards."

An article in the *Carolina Watchman* published in March of 1863 posed a critical question, then answered it:

> What, then, have they to support life? Bread and water! Bread is the only thing with their limited means they could provide for themselves; and at present prices, it is not very easy for even the industrious poor to provide this. They certainly cannot afford to buy flour at $50 per barrel.

To make matters worse, speculators also hoarded thread and fabric. Many women earned a meager living sewing uniforms for the army, and when they were not able to procure materials, they could not work. Clearly it was time to take action.

According to Salisbury's daily newspaper *Carolina Watchman*, it was "one of the gayest and liveliest scenes of the age." Salisbury merchant Michael Brown took a different view, lamenting in a letter to Governor Vance, "No resistance was offered, no effort made to end and prohibit the illegal and forcible seizure." Mrs. Mary C. Moore of Salisbury provided yet another perspective. She wrote to Governor Vance, "Having from absolute necessity been forced into measures not at all pleasant to obtain something to eat . . . we then forced our way in and compelled them to give us something."

At about two o'clock on March 18, 1863, between forty and fifty women assembled, many carrying hatchets or axes. They had no intention of using these implements on people but realized it might be necessary to hack their way into barrels or warehouses.

Indeed, the tools proved handy at their very first stop—the business of Michael Brown. Brown refused to sell them his flour for what they offered—$19.50 per barrel—claiming he had paid more than twice that sum for it. In a letter to Governor Vance, Brown fumed:

> A few hours ago a mob of females . . . appeared in front of my business and demanded my flour. Some were armed with hatchets with which they broke the knob of the door and cut away a portion of the door itself. After remonstrating with them they agreed to disperse after the delivery of *ten barrels* of flour.

To Brown, the most appalling aspect of the incident was the fact that the mayor and some of the commissioners of the town were present—and did nothing. The ladies next approached John Ennis and were given three barrels of flour without argument.

Subsequently, H. Sprague gave the women a barrel of molasses, and David Weil and Thomas Foster each donated a sack of salt. Finally, the women headed for the North Carolina Central Railroad Depot in Salisbury, where they believed flour belonging to David Weil was stored. The railroad agent balked, protesting that the flour was actually the property of a man from Charlotte. Demonstrating uncommon courage (or foolhardiness), the agent declared, "Ladies, it is useless to attempt it, unless you go in over my dead body." In his 1983 article for *The State*, Tom F. Skipper commented:

> This was evidently satisfactory to the women, for the newspaper reports that "A rush was made, and in they went, and the last I saw of the agent, he was sitting on a log blowing like a March wind." The ladies took 10 barrels of flour and rolled them out of the storehouse.

The *Carolina Watchman* sympathized with the plight of the women but cautioned against such activities in general:

> The experiment of "impressment" is a very dangerous one, and must, if persisted in, lead to the gravest consequences imaginable. In the first place, it is unjust to the few whose property is taken . . . . Many a speculator whom you did not visit is as guilty as those you did visit . . . . All should be treated alike. But how will you do this? Without equality there will be just cause of complaint, there will be bitterness of feeling, and speedily we shall see wrangling, and deadly strifes amongst ourselves, for these are the fruits of lawless proceedings.

In April of 1863, not long after the Salisbury raid, a group of Greensboro women were arrested for similar behavior. According to a letter written by Nancy Mangum to Governor Vance, the jailed women were told they would be fed with "dog meet and Roten egges."

To his credit and to the relief of the war's most vulnerable victims, Governor Vance took action on their behalf. According to Skipper:

On April 13, 1863 [Vance] issued a proclamation making it illegal to export foodstuffs and cloth out of the state for the space of 30 days. The proclamation was extended numerous times, making it in effect a permanent ban on exports.

The Stranger from New Orleans
· 1865 ·

For more than four years the Civil War had raged. It seemed clear the South was doomed, but the fighting continued, with both armies entrenched around Petersburg. In the hills of western North Carolina, a rumor began to spread that the Yankees were planning to invade the region.

Not long after Wallace Reinhardt of Lincolnton got word of the possible assault, he received an urgent message from his friend and fellow resident, a Frenchman named Lorendzo Ferrier. Ferrier wanted to move his valuables to the Lincoln County Courthouse vault for safekeeping. As Reinhardt helped his friend load his three iron treasure chests onto a wagon, he thought about the theory he had begun to form about Ferrier's true identity.

The tall, dark-haired, handsome Ferrier had arrived in town about twenty years earlier under a cloud of mystery, accompanied by a strikingly attractive young woman of African descent. As the couple rode down the street in their fine carriage, the people of Lincolnton stood in doorways and on corners, watching and wondering. Even more intriguing to them than the dashing man and his lady were the three huge iron chests stacked on the back of the buggy.

The man introduced himself as Lorendzo Ferrier from New Orleans. His beautiful companion and housekeeper, Louisa, was one-eighth African, an ancestral blend known as "octoroon." Ferrier set up residence in a two-story house near the Lincoln County jail.

Although he and Louisa led a largely secluded life, they were occasionally seen riding down the main street in Ferrier's carriage. Over the years the stranger from New Orleans bought property in several locations in the town and county, including an acreage three miles north of Lincolnton he later donated to St. Paul's Episcopal Church. In 1858, Louisa passed away. She was buried in St. Luke's churchyard. The following inscription was carved on her tombstone:

> To the memory of Louisa, born in Richmond, Va. Died November 29, 1858. Aged 40 years. The deceased was amiable, kind and pious. She was in life respected and in death lamented by all who knew her. The marble monument will crumble and decay, but the virtues of the deceased will live forever. This token to the memory of the deceased is erected by her Master L. Ferrier.

Those who met the charming Lorendzo Ferrier could tell that he was of French descent and very wealthy, yet there was much they could not discern. For example, he seemed not to be of any particular profession, and his family background was not known. He never offered an explanation for how he came by his money.

But Wallace Reinhardt had his suspicions. When he and Ferrier arrived at the courthouse in 1865 to secure the Frenchman's valuables, he received further evidence to support his belief. More than a century later, Lincolnton resident and writer Gladys Childs described the scene for readers of *The State* in her article, "The Pirate Who Came to Lincolnton":

> Opening one of the chests, Ferrier scooped up a double handful of gold coins, and gave them to Reinhardt for services rendered. He also gave Reinhardt a handsome massive gold watch attached to a heavy gold chain.

Reinhardt could think of only one occupation that might yield riches like those Ferrier possessed. The fact that Ferrier said he was from New Orleans added another interesting piece to the puzzle. Reinhardt recalled that another tall, dashing, dark-haired man had earned a somewhat mixed reputation in Louisiana in the early 1800s. That man's name was Jean Lafitte.

At various times, Lafitte was called "The Corsair," "The Buccaneer," "The King of Barataria," "The Terror of the Gulf," and "The Hero of New Orleans." Condemned for his actions more than once by U.S. presidents, he was nonetheless lauded by General Andrew Jackson for the critical part he played in defeating the British at the Battle of New Orleans.

Contrary to the image painted by his detractors, Jean Lafitte did not consider himself a pirate. He preferred the term "corsair" or "privateer." Proud of the fact that he had never authorized an attack on an American ship, he constantly stressed to his men that America was worth defending with their last drop of blood. Lafitte was well read, well dressed, and cultured, the sort of person who always found himself welcome in polite society. Even so, he was not able to completely withdraw from his chosen profession, and eventually he was forced to leave New Orleans.

In 1817, Lafitte fled to Texas. On Galveston Island, he built a two-story brick home that doubled as a fort. According to Joseph Geringer in "Jean Lafitte: Gentleman Pirate of New Orleans," the set-up

> offered excellent living quarters and rooms in which to entertain business partners, as well as a barracks for his men. Cannon barrels protruded from its upper port-holes over the Gulf. Around it sprang the warehouses of trade, a slave quarters, cattle pens, taverns and frame cottages of his crew.

By 1820, Lafitte was in trouble again. It seemed that his harassment of Spanish ships off the American coast was interfering with President James Madison's efforts to establish peaceful relations with Spain. Threatened with total destruction if he did not vacate the island, the gentleman pirate departed in 1821, after first setting fire to his settlement. No one ever knew for sure where he went from there—but Wallace Reinhardt of Lincolnton, North Carolina, thought he had a pretty good idea. He wasn't the only one. According to Childs:

> The late George Kizer, who was up in years when I came to Lincolnton, said in his boyhood he and his buddies would gather around Ferrier on the Court Square and listen to the fascinating stories he told of piracy. The boys called him "The Pirate." He let them see and handle the coins and jewels in his treasure chests.

Ferrier lived to be ninety-six. In his lengthy will, he dealt generously with his friends and servants. A granite-topped, six-legged table monument stands in the midst of the square, round, and peaked tombstones in St. Luke's churchyard. The inscription reads: "Lorendzo Ferrier, born in the city of Lyons died on the 16th of April, 1875, aged 96 years."

Was Lorendzo Ferrier really Jean Lafitte, the notorious pirate who once commanded a vast fleet of vessels and presided over a three-island kingdom called Barataria in the Gulf of Mexico? Wallace Reinhardt firmly believed he was. More than a hundred years later, Reinhardt's descendants proudly display Ferrier's old inkwell made of solid lead—2 I inches wide at the base, weighing 4 G pounds—the type of inkwell used by ship captains in days gone by. It is an everlasting reminder that once upon a time, an infamous pirate may have lived in Lincoln County, North Carolina.

Everything Is Dark
·1865·

The whole earth seemed stricken with grief. Heavy rains had already saturated the ground, yet the sky still wept as if heartbroken. Shrouded in somber clouds, the sun offered no consolation. Spring was supposed to be a season of joy and rebirth, but such sentiments had no place in the procession of men, horses, wagons, and carriages that pulled out of Greensboro, North Carolina, the morning of April 14, 1865.

Sticky red clay mud sucked at the wheels of the vehicles in the dismal parade. More than once a member of the convoy had to be pulled or pushed out of a sinkhole. Slowly and sadly the group slogged its way south toward Charlotte. As the darkness grew deeper, the only light marking the passage of the caravan came from the glowing tip of a cigar belonging to one of the men on horseback. His name was Judah Benjamin. From time to time, he removed the cigar to intone words from Tennyson's "Ode on the Death of the Duke of Wellington":

Bury the Great Duke
With an empire's lamentation;
Let us bury the Great Duke
To the noise of the mourning of a mighty nation;
Mourning when their leaders fall,
Warriors carry the warrior's pall,
And sorrow darkens hamlet and hall.

Although the cortege carried no coffin, in many ways it still qualified as a funeral procession. Death was everywhere. Benjamin had seen it blazing in the eyes of the thieves who roved the streets of Greensboro, stealing horses and raiding stores; had seen it flash from the guns of the home guards protecting the supplies; had seen it staring from the thin, ghostly faces of women and children who longed for the end of war. He saw it in each step taken by the old, broken-down horses who struggled to keep the caravan moving.

Judah Benjamin was a man of high office, having been appointed secretary of state in 1862. Riding next to him on a worn and weary steed was the person who had named him to that position: Jefferson Davis, president of the Confederate States of America (CSA). Even though Davis and the others in the entourage were very much alive, the Confederate cause lay fatally wounded, on the brink of total starvation. As far as Benjamin was concerned, it was already dead. Davis had not yet given up hope but had recently expressed concern in a letter to his wife: "I will come to you if I can—Everything is dark—you should prepare for the worst. . . . My love to the children and Maggie—God bless, guide and preserve you."

An owl hooted from the woods nearby. Benjamin's horse snorted and tipped its ears forward.

Not only were Davis and the other officers of the Confederate government in mourning, they were in danger as well. Union raiders might catch up with them at any moment. Forced to flee Richmond on April 2 to avoid capture by the Federals, they had traveled south to Danville, Virginia, by train. It was the only route of escape still open.

Davis had sent his wife and family away the previous month. "If I live," he told his wife at that time, "you can come to me when the struggle is ended, but I do not expect to survive the destruction of constitutional liberty."

Arriving in Danville on Monday, April 3, Davis was received in the home of Mr. and Mrs. Sutherlin. On Tuesday he met with his cabinet members to draft a proclamation to the people of the Confederacy. In part it read:

> We have now entered upon a new phase of the struggle . . . . Nothing is needed to render our triumph certain, but the exhibition of our own unquenchable resolve. . . . I will never consent to abandon to the enemy one foot of the soil of any of the States of the Confederacy . . . again and again we will return.

That same day, President Abraham Lincoln arrived in the former capital of the CSA. Even as Davis prepared his proclamation 140 miles away, Lincoln was walking through the Confederate president's Richmond home, now General Weitzel's headquarters. He went into Davis's office and sat in his chair, deep in thought, trying to determine how to deal with the fallen leaders of the Confederacy.

Meanwhile, Davis still had faith that the troops could be rallied. He and General Robert E. Lee had agreed that if Lee had to evacuate Petersburg, he would proceed to Danville to make a new defensive line of attack. On Monday morning, April 10, Davis anxiously awaited word from Lee concerning the execution of this plan. He received unwelcome news: Lee had surrendered to General Ulysses S. Grant at Appomattox Court House the previous afternoon.

Davis knew he and his cabinet must leave Danville. After studying a map, he determined that Charlotte, North Carolina, would be a safe haven for the time being. They would travel by way of Greensboro.

In Greensboro the Davis entourage was not well received. In an article for *Century Magazine* published in 1883, Davis's private secretary Burton N. Harrison wrote:

> It was rarely that anybody asked one of us to his house; and but few of them had the grace even to explain their

fear that, if they entertained us, their houses would be burned by the enemy, when his cavalry got there.

The presidential party set up headquarters in a broken-down, leaky railroad car. Davis was given a bed in a small second-floor apartment in the home of John Taylor Wood. Ailing treasury secretary George Trenholm found lodging in the mansion of John M. Morehead, a former North Carolina governor. At the Wood residence on April 12 and 13, the Confederate cabinet conferred. Those present included Secretary of the Navy Stephen R. Mallory; John Reagan, postmaster general; Judah Benjamin; staff-officers; and Generals Joseph E. Johnston and P.G.T. Beauregard. General John C. Breckinridge, secretary of war, personally delivered confirmation of Lee's surrender.

As Jefferson Davis rode through the night toward Charlotte two days later, he couldn't help recalling Johnston's words and his spiteful tone of voice. "It would be the greatest of human crimes for us to attempt to continue the war," Johnston had said. With the exception of Benjamin, every man in the room had agreed.

As a result, a proposal was now on its way to Union General William T. Sherman. The document suggested "a temporary suspension of active operations" so that the opposing factions could "enter into the needful arrangements to terminate the existing war." On April 13 or 14, Davis received an official message from Lee detailing his surrender. This tangible evidence of the demise of the CSA hit the Confederate leader with the force of a physical blow.

Now the fugitive government plodded along a muddy road in the dead of night. An escort of Tennessee and Kentucky cavalry had joined the group in Greensboro to help protect Davis en route to Charlotte. Exhausted after traveling just ten miles, the group stopped in Jamestown for the night. While they slept, Abraham Lincoln was assassinated in Washington. Completely cut off from communication, the members of the Davis caravan journeyed on from Jamestown through High Point, Lexington, Salisbury, and

Concord. They did not receive word of Lincoln's assassination until they reached Charlotte on April 19.

Davis heard the news as he stood outside the home of his host, Lewis Bates, superintendent of the Southern Express Company. A crowd had gathered and called on the Confederate president to speak. Accounts of Davis's reaction to Lincoln's death differ. Bates testified that Davis was pleased with the news. However, all other witnesses stated that he expressed regret, calling the event "lamentable" and "awful."

In Charlotte, the Davis administration discussed Sherman's counterproposal, delivered by Breckinridge. The cabinet found the provisions not only acceptable but remarkably favorable. Davis did not share their optimism, primarily because he strongly suspected the federal authorities would reject the agreement. He was right.

At noon on Wednesday, April 26, Johnston surrendered to Sherman in Charlotte. Close to that same time, accompanied by approximately three thousand cavalrymen, his staff, and cabinet members, Davis left the town he had hoped would become the new capital of the CSA. He was eventually captured in Georgia and imprisoned for two years, then released without trial.

Many states claim a connection with Jefferson Davis. Born in Kentucky, he spent much of his life in Mississippi. He died in Louisiana and is buried in Virginia. Yet, all things considered, perhaps one of the most profound periods of his life happened in a state not usually associated with his name. It was in North Carolina that Davis began to relinquish one of the most significant roles in the history of the United States, a role he had not sought but had fulfilled to the best of his ability. In North Carolina he was forced to face the beginning of the end of the CSA as across the nation, men laid down their weapons. America was about to be reborn.

A King in His Pride
· 1880 ·

The circus! The circus! The throb of the drums,
And the blare of the horns as the band-wagon comes;
The clash and the clang of the cymbals that beat,
As the glittering pageant winds down the long street!

And the elephant, too (with his undulant stride
That rocks the high throne of a king in his pride),
That in jungles of India shook from his flanks
The tiger that leapt from the Jujubee banks.

Attributed to James Whitcomb Riley, the above lines capture
the excitement experienced by anyone who has encountered the
sounds, sights, and smells of a circus parade. Riley's poem
appeared in a book commemorating the 100th Annual Tour of
John Robinson's Circus, a great "amusement enterprise" first
organized in 1824. Riley, who died in 1916, was privileged to live
in the "Golden Age" of the American circus. The number of great
circuses that existed during that period—from the late 1800s into
the 1920s—has never been equaled.

The circus as a form of entertainment was introduced in the
United States in the 1790s. Early shows primarily featured trained
horses and equestrian performances. During the first few decades
of the 1800s, rope dancing, juggling, acrobatic acts, wild animal
acts, and clowning were introduced. Before long, one animal in

particular became a bigger star than almost any other—literally and figuratively. By the 1880s many circuses had one key objective: to exhibit more elephants than their competitors.

But the John Robinson Circus didn't go in for big elephant herds. In fact the Robinsons boasted only three elephants in the fall of 1880 when their troupe played Charlotte, North Carolina. As it turned out, they had one elephant too many.

At about eight o'clock on the night of September 27, 1880, a large crowd gathered near the Trade Street railroad crossing in Charlotte. The Robinsons' main animal keeper, a powerfully built man named John King, was unloading his elephants: Chief, Mary, and "The Boy." Chief, an adult bull and the largest of the three, was the first to emerge from his railroad car. King seemed to have a special rapport with Chief. In fact, he considered the huge gray beast his pet.

Chief was probably an Indian elephant and, as such, might easily have been ten feet high. He could have weighed as much as eleven thousand pounds. As he shuffled down the ramp, he displayed the peaceful, easygoing demeanor common to most elephants. Thanks to their enormous size and thick, tough skin, they have few enemies to fear. Nevertheless, as an experienced elephant handler, John King knew that once male elephants reach puberty they become unpredictable. It always made him nervous when townspeople got too close to Chief.

"Look out there!" he shouted to the crowd. "If that elephant hits any of you all, I'll not be responsible for it."

King knew Chief occasionally became unruly. About ten years earlier he had been in a terrible fight near Louisa Court House, Virginia. An account of the incident was provided by Richard E. Conover in his book *Give 'Em a John Robinson*:

There was eight elephants involved: Emperor . . . Chief, Princess, and Mary . . . and four unaccountable others—Radjak, Caliph, Woodah, and Bismark, the latter and Princess being of the African species. Chief was credited with starting the melee by attacking Bismark; but, before it was over, the rest of the eight took sides.

When Chief acted up, King could usually count on Mary to settle him down. In elephant society, mature females carry a lot of clout. Many an elephant trainer has subdued a misbehaving bull simply by leading a ranking cow into view.

That night in Charlotte, after issuing his warning to the crowd, King stepped around to Chief's head, intending to turn him around. Witnesses later said that suddenly they heard King call the elephant by name in a frightened tone. On September 28 the *Charlotte Observer* reported:

> The next moment they saw the enraged animal turn upon his keeper and crush him against the car. King sank to the ground without a groan and the men who were with him fled precipitately. The crowd scattered up Trade street and the wildest confusion followed. . . . The elephant surveyed the scene for an instant, gave a short snort and started at brisk pace up the railroad track.

King was taken across the street to a barber shop and doctors were summoned. Chief ambled up the track in smooth, rhythmic strides and disappeared into the night. Word of his escape quickly spread through the town.

Before long some of King's coworkers set out after the fugitive, with Mary and The Boy in tow. On arriving at the next crossing Chief turned up Fifth Street. He stopped for a moment at Tryon, then went directly across to Church Street. There he was apprehended and chained to the other two elephants.

En route back to the circus train, the trio of pachyderms decided to stop at a pump for a drink of water. According to the *Charlotte Observer:*

In the movements about the pump the chains became entangled, and the three began to move round and round drawing them gradually together. Chief's temper was again aroused and he began to bellow. The wild, weird noise threw panic into the crowd and there was a confused retreat.

It is difficult to say what caused Chief's behavior. Elephant experts now know that once a year male elephants go through a period called musth. During this time the bull's testosterone levels increase dramatically. Musth can come on very suddenly and temperament can change in less than fifteen minutes. When a bull "goes musth," he may trample down everything in his path.

John King died the morning of September 28 at about eleven o'clock. He was buried in Charlotte that afternoon. A hearse drawn by four white horses carried his casket to the graveyard. Mary and The Boy followed solemnly, their gait stately and respectful. According to the *Observer*, John Lowlow, a veteran clown with the Robinson circus, said "that King was somewhat to blame for the animal's viciousness as he never would consent to any violent measures to subdue him."

On October 1, 1880, the *Observer* reported that Chief was "rapidly growing more vicious and unruly" and the Robinsons were making plans to donate him to the Zoological Gardens in Cincinnati and "in the event of failing to get him a berth there, to kill him, as he has become useless to them." According to Richard E. Conover in *Give 'Em a John Robinson,* "Chief . . . was finally placed in the Cincinnati Zoo. . . ."

Although the poem published in the Robinsons' 100th Annual Tour Book focused on the "gleam and the glint and the glamour and glare" of circus life, sorrows and hardships have always been as common in that world as anywhere else. People take comfort in gathering to mourn the passing of a friend. John Robinson's route book contained the following notation under "Charlotte, N.C., Thursday, October 3, 1901":

After the matinee, a number of the company, including John G. Robinson, paid the customary visit to the grave of John King, who was killed by the elephant "Chief" in that city in 1880. Floral tributes were laid on the grave, and after a rendition of "Nearer, My God, to Thee," by the circus band, Ed C. Cullen, in well selected words, delivered an appropriate address to the party.

"This Last and Most Wonderful Discovery of the Century"
· 1898 ·

Six-year-old Ellen Harris of Harrisburg, North Carolina, lay as still as death, her skin pale, her body pitifully thin, her throat horribly swollen. She could not eat or speak. Silently she stared at the wall as the clock struck midnight and a new year—1898—dawned crisp and cold.

In November Ellen had swallowed a brass thimble, and it had apparently lodged in her throat. Doctors had tried to remove it several times without success. Meanwhile, Ellen had grown weaker and weaker, eventually developing tonsillitis and bronchitis. Her parents, Mr. and Mrs. Will Harris, had begun to fear they would lose their precious child.

Hope was fading rapidly when the Harrises suddenly remembered something they had read in the *Charlotte Observer*. It was a long shot, but one they could ill afford to reject. They decided to contact Dr. Henry Louis Smith at Davidson College.

Dr. Smith, a native of Greensboro, North Carolina, had been a professor of physics and astronomy at Davidson for more than ten years. In January of 1896, his life had taken a dramatic turn when a news item caught his eye:

It is announced that Professor [Wilhelm] Roentgen of the Wurzburg University has discovered a light which for the purpose of photography will penetrate wood, flesh, cloth, and most other organic substances. The Professor has succeeded in photographing metal weights which were in a closed wooden case, also a man's hand which showed only the bones, the flesh being invisible.

On January 24, an English translation of Roentgen's manuscript "A New Kind of Ray, A Preliminary Communication" was published, introducing America to the X-ray. Dr. Smith soon realized that he had the same type of equipment in his own laboratory that Roentgen had used to discover the X-ray. His response was described in *Presbyterian Hospital, The Spirit of Caring, 1903–1985:*

[Smith] got to work. He cut off the hand of a cadaver, then shot it with a .22 caliber ball. He then took an X-ray picture of the hand which showed the bullet firmly embedded in the cadaver's hand. This was one of the first X-ray photographs ever taken in the South.

Mr. and Mrs. Harris remembered reading about Dr. Smith's experiment. Perhaps, they reasoned, this incredible X-ray machine could locate the thimble stuck in Ellen's throat.

Dr. Smith didn't have to be asked twice for a chance to show what his equipment could do. He loaded the storage batteries, induction coil, a Crookes' tube, and a small hand fluoroscope into a horsedrawn hack sent by the Harris family. On a frosty morning in early January, he traveled twenty-five miles to the Harris residence. The *Daily Concord Standard* filed this report on January 5, 1898:

Dr. Smith of Davidson College is at the home of Mr. Will Harris of No. 1 township today to take an X-ray observation of the thimble swallowed by Mr. Harris' little girl some time ago. We could not learn of the particulars.

The "particulars" were not for the faint of heart. Ellen Harris was emaciated. Five doctors stood around her bed. Three claimed that she had not swallowed the thimble but instead had a progressive throat disease. The other two physicians agreed that she had swallowed the thimble but couldn't decide whether it was in her throat or her stomach. Dr. Smith described what happened next:

We swung her in a heavy sheet far off the floor and using a fluoroscope, crouched under her body. I spent an hour with my crude apparatus trying to pick out the thimble, in spite of the heavy vertebrae of the backbone. At last for a fleeting moment I saw it with perfect distinctness when the electric action was unusually good, and was perfectly sure of the correctness of the vision.

The *Daily Concord Standard* heralded the news on January 7:

HE FOUND IT! Dr. Henry Louis Smith, of Davidson college, brought his X-ray apparatus yesterday afternoon to Mr. Will E. Harris' and after looking all through the body of his little girl, found the thimble in the back part of her lung, about an inch to the left of the backbone. The doctor was about to conclude the thimble was not in the body when he decided to look through the back. He at once found it distinctly visible, lying with the small end towards the shoulder.

His mission accomplished, Dr. Smith returned to Davidson— only to be summoned back to Charlotte the next day. Ellen Harris was in the hospital awaiting surgery to remove the thimble, but the surgeons wanted to see the object themselves before proceeding with the operation.

Dr. Smith was never able to get the surgeons to see the thimble, but he saw it so clearly, he eventually convinced them of where it was. They lowered a flexible steel tube down Ellen's esophagus while Dr. Smith watched to see if it would pass through the thimble. It missed, and the doctors then knew the thimble was lodged in the child's windpipe.

On the morning of January 9, Dr. John R. Irwin of Mecklenburg County administered chloroform to Ellen Harris. This in itself was hazardous. In Ellen's weakened condition, she might not have been able to recover from the effects.

Around ten o'clock, Dr. C. A. Misenheimer, a native of Cabarrus County, made an incision in Ellen's windpipe, just above the breastbone and an inch below her larynx. As soon as the larynx was opened, an instrument was passed into her trachea.

"I feel it," Dr. Misenheimer said as he touched the thimble.

The operation lasted about forty-five minutes. The *Charlotte Observer* reported that the walls of the child's trachea had grown over the edges of the thimble, making removal extremely difficult. Finally, Dr. Misenheimer managed to pull the object out. According to the *Observer*:

> It was difficult to say who was the happiest of that, an hour before, unhappy family—the anxious parents, the hospital surgeons, or Dr. Smith. To each the operation meant much—to the parents a loved child restored; to the physicians the success of a dangerous operation which only skilled hands could perform; to Dr. Smith the triumph of the new discovery in science, which he was the first in the South to use.

Not long after his success in Charlotte, Dr. Smith was called in on another case. On Christmas Day, ten-year-old Jennie Lewis of Wilmington had swallowed a piece of a hat pin. Dr. Smith located the pin on January 12 and two successive surgeries were performed on the girl in an attempt to remove the pin fragment from her lung. Details were not published, but the *Observer* reported that she returned home on January 22.

On January 24 Dr. Smith presented a lecture called "The X-Rays" to the general public in Charlotte. After the lecture, many in the audience gathered around the X-ray machine to view the bones in their own hands. In an article about the presentation, the *Observer* described the new medical miracle as "this last and most wonderful discovery of the century."

No one agreed more than the family of Ellen Harris.

Flight of Fancy
· 1903 ·

At about ten o'clock in the morning on December 17, 1903, John T. Daniels stepped out of the lifesaving station at Kill Devil Hills, four miles from Kitty Hawk, North Carolina. The surf boiled in a roaring white foam. According to the station's anemometer, the icy winds were gusting to twenty-seven miles per hour. A lone seagull passed overhead, beating its wings frantically in a vain effort to fly upright. As Daniels knew well, winter never minced words when she announced her arrival on the Outer Banks.

Suddenly he gasped in disbelief, nearly dropping his cup of steaming coffee. Out at the Wright brothers' campsite, a white flag flapped wildly from a post. Surely those boys from Ohio weren't planning to take that clumsy flying machine up today! But the signal was unmistakable.

Daniels and four other men hurried to join the brothers. Wilbur and Orville Wright had already begun laying their sixty-foot sectional track. It was so cold they had to duck into their cabin at intervals to warm their hands over a stove. By half past ten, the men had maneuvered the Flyer into place on a truck, facing directly into the north wind. Daniels stepped back, fascinated. He estimated that the contraption was a little more than twenty-one feet long, with a wingspan of about forty feet. Wilbur cranked the lightweight motor he and Orville had designed, and it clattered to life.

The two brothers walked some distance away. They talked for a few minutes, their oddly formal clothing flapping in the wind.

Daniels had never seen them wear anything but gentlemen's attire: suitcoats and trousers, stiff-collared white shirts, and vests.

Although their manner of dress was similar, Wilbur and Orville were unlike each other in many ways. Wilbur, older by four years, was slim and angular, lean-faced, with piercing blue-gray eyes. Intense and analytical, he kept to himself much of the time. In contrast, Orville never hesitated to greet a stranger. Shorter than Wilbur and a bit heavier, he seemed to have boundless energy and enthusiasm. Where Wilbur was nearly bald, Orville had a full head of dark hair and a neatly trimmed mustache to match.

The brothers finished their conversation and shook hands. To Daniels, it seemed that they held on a bit long, like people who think they may not ever see each other again. Indeed, Daniels noted, they were taking a huge risk. More than one brave soul had met his death attempting to conquer the skies, and today's conditions were especially dangerous.

Yet the Wrights were confident they would succeed. Just three days earlier, Wilbur had stayed in the air for about four seconds, traveling more than one hundred feet. The next day the brothers had worked until dark to repair a damaged rudder. Exhausted, they had retired to the sturdy wooden building they had constructed. That night, as Wilbur settled into a cot that hung from the rafters, he recalled what the campsite had been like during their earliest visits to Kitty Hawk in 1900 and 1901. He and Orville had slept in a tent, fearing for their lives every time a roaring "noreaster" threatened to lift their flimsy abode off the ground.

In Ohio, they had lived in comfort, but Wilbur had been bored senseless running a printing business and, later, a bicycle repair shop. Kitty Hawk was far more primitive than Dayton, but it was the perfect place to test a flying machine.

"There are neither hills nor trees, so that it offers a safe place for practice," Wilbur had written his father in September of 1901. "Also, the wind there is stronger than any place near home and is almost constant."

In their quest to conquer the sky, Wilbur knew he and Orville must prove themselves more capable than aviation giants like Sir Hiram Maxim, Otto Lilienthal, Octave Chanute, and Samuel Langley. About a week ago, Langley's most recent attempt at flight had failed. The Wrights knew winter was closing in, so if they didn't take the Flyer on another trial run soon, they were done for the season.

In his diary entry for December 17, 1903, Orville wrote: "When we got up, a wind of between 20 and 25 miles was blowing from the north. We got the machine out early and put out the sign for the men at the station."

After the brothers shook hands, Orville climbed aboard the Flyer and positioned himself carefully in the hip cradle, left of center. In that position, he balanced the engine, located right of center. The motor sputtered, and the spinning propeller blades whirred. Orville released the restraining wire. The Flyer started forward. Wilbur ran alongside for about forty feet, his hand on the right wingtip struts to balance the craft. As the machine lifted from its track, Daniels caught the moment on film.

Squinting into the relentless, icy headwind, Orville struggled to control the front rudder. The Flyer tilted to the left. He righted it. No matter what happened, he must not let the craft go too high in such strong, irregular winds. Alternately rising and dipping, the aircraft skimmed above the earth, then slid to a halt in the sand.

In Orville's words, "This flight lasted only twelve seconds, but it was nevertheless the first in the history of the world in which a machine carrying a man had raised itself by its own power into the air in full flight, had sailed forward without reduction of speed, and had finally landed at a point as high as that from which it started."

On the next run, Wilbur bettered Orville's distance. They lugged the Flyer back to the rail and set up again. Orville's second attempt took him to a height of more than fifteen feet. As he rose, the right wing tilted sharply, and a sudden gust of wind turned the machine sideways. The men on the ground gasped in horror. To their relief, Orville steadied the craft and brought it down safely about two hundred feet from takeoff.

At noon Wilbur settled himself in the hip cradle and prepared for trial number four of the day. Right away he had problems. The machine rose and dipped alarmingly. Fighting to control the bucking aircraft with a combination of mental determination and physical force, he passed the two-hundred-foot mark, then three hundred, then four hundred. He was almost level. Cruising ten feet above the sand, the Flyer bored straight into the wind. Wilbur Wright was flying!

Soon, however, the machine began to pitch again. The skids hit the sand and the Flyer came to a stop. Whooping and hollering, Orville and the others rushed to Wilbur's side. He had flown 852 feet in just under one minute.

Several hours later, Bishop Milton Wright entered the parlor of his home in Dayton, a telegram from his son Orville in his hands. The bishop's daughter, Katharine, looked up from her book.

"Success," Bishop Wright read aloud. "Four flights Thursday morning all against twenty-one mile wind. Started from level with engine power alone. Average speed through air thirty-one miles. Longest 57 seconds. Inform Press. Home Christmas."

"I knew they could do it!" Katharine declared.

To her, Wilbur and Orville's project had always been more than a mere "flight of fancy," a leap into the world of make believe. Her speaking and writing campaign had been instrumental in raising funds for their work.

Later, she and her father learned the flight had actually lasted fifty-nine seconds, not fifty-seven. An even greater error was made by a Dayton's Associated Press representative. He did not consider the flight newsworthy. If it had lasted fifty-seven *minutes*, he said, he might have covered it.

Fortunately, his failure to appreciate the importance of the event mattered scarcely at all. Before long the story he declined to run was printed permanently on the pages of history. The age of aviation had arrived.

Batter Up!
·1914·

T he kid from Baltimore had talent, no doubt about it. He could catch, pitch, hit, and play third base—all extremely well. In one high school game, he had struck out six men, doubled, tripled, and scored the only home run of the contest.

But that was high school. This was professional baseball. The kid had just been signed by the Baltimore Orioles, a newly formed minor league franchise, at a salary of one hundred dollars per week. He would have to prove himself to the rest of the club, many of them seasoned veterans.

Jack Dunn, owner and manager of the Orioles, prided himself on being able to spot young athletes with potential. A lot of eyes would be watching the kid, a twenty-year-old, six-foot-two, 180-pound rookie who had spent the past ten years at St. Mary's Industrial School for Boys.

Blizzard conditions prevailed in Baltimore the night of March 2, 1914. It was the worst storm the city had seen in twenty-five years. On Tuesday morning, March 3, twelve members of the Orioles team slogged through snow-filled, debris-clogged streets to Union Station and hopped a train for Fayetteville, North Carolina. Spring training camp was about to begin. "The Birds Have Migrated," announced the *Fayetteville Observer*, describing the team members as "fine looking sturdy young fellows" who seemed "fit and ready for the fray."

But if the Orioles expected to be greeted by warm weather in the "sunny South," they were destined for disappointment. Temperatures in Fayetteville were barely above freezing when they arrived. The dampness in the air settled into their bones the minute they stepped off the train.

Scout Steinmann, ex-ballplayer, coach, and all-around handyman, grumbled as he herded his charges into the Lafayette Hotel. Prospects looked pretty bleak for practicing.

By midday, the sun had come out and the temperature was on its way up. Steinmann took the team to the fairgrounds for a workout. He told the rangy rookie from Baltimore to throw a few and watched him whip the ball across the diamond. With his broad shoulders and long arms, he could throw hard and fast, but he was obviously showing off. Steinmann yelled at him to let up and take it easy. There was no sense in overdoing things the first day of camp.

The weather cooperated the next day. In the hot Fayetteville sun, the players practiced batting and hit fly balls to the outfield. Thursday, it rained. Team members were in the armory throwing baseballs when catcher Ben Egan arrived. Tall, cheerful, and full of fire, Egan always energized the group, and they were glad to see him.

On Friday, the rain continued. The first practice game of the season had been set for the next day, Saturday, but it looked like the field would be too soggy to use, even if the weather cleared. To everyone's amazement, Saturday brought a warm sun and brisk wind. Soon the field was dry.

Egan and Steinmann divided the squad into two teams for a seven-inning scrub game. Steinmann called his team the Sparrows. He put himself at first base. He was able to assign a pitcher to pitch and a catcher to catch, but the rest of the lineup left something to be desired. Veteran pitcher Dave Danforth was at second. A catcher played shortstop; a pitcher was at third base. Three pitchers stood in the outfield.

The Buzzards, Egan's team, also had a pitcher and catcher in their correct positions. Egan was on first base, with veteran pitcher Lefty Cottrell at second. One of the rookies played third base. In the outfield the Buzzards boasted pitcher "Smoke"

Klingelhoefer in left, a reporter from the *Baltimore News* in center, and another pitcher in right. Egan put the kid from St. Mary's at shortstop.

By the start of the first inning, a crowd of nearly two hundred townspeople had gathered for a glimpse of the pros in action. The Buzzards scored a run in the top of the first, and the Sparrows tied it in the bottom. With the bases loaded in the top of the second, Egan hit a double that scored three runs. Cottrell singled, scoring Egan. What happened next was destined to go down as one of baseball history's "moments to remember."

The kid from St. Mary's stepped up to the plate, cocked his bat over his shoulder, set his jaw, and waited. The pitch hummed toward him. He swung, and bat met ball with a resounding "crack!" The spectators gasped. Four years ago, in 1910, Jim Thorpe had hit the longest home run ever seen at the fairgrounds. This guy with the Orioles had just hit a homer at least sixty feet beyond Thorpe's.

As Roger Pippen, the newspaperman playing centerfield, wrote in a story for the *Baltimore News*, "The ball carried so far to right field that he walked around the bases." Another sports reporter later wrote that the youth swung at the ball in much the same manner as Joe Jackson, universally touted as a great natural hitter.

As the rangy rookie from Baltimore headed for the dugout, he couldn't help being pleased that he was doing so well in his first game as a professional. After five innings at shortstop, he took the pitcher's mound, where he delivered a series of hopping fastballs with the greatest of ease. The Buzzards won 15 to 9.

"This boy is the prize beauty of the rookies in camp," raved the sports pages. When Orioles manager Jack Dunn arrived in Fayetteville the next day, he found the place buzzing over the big, overgrown kid who could out-hit Jim Thorpe. Dunn watched him play and immediately joined the fan club.

"He has all the earmarks of a great ballplayer," Dunn said. "He hits like a fiend and he seems to be at home in any position, even though he's lefthanded. He's the most promising young ballplayer I've ever had."

Not everyone on the team was thrilled. On one occasion, when Dunn arrived at the field with the rookie, another player taunted the kid, calling out, "Well, here's Jack's newest babe!" He got a laugh. And the kid from St. Mary's got a nickname he would never shed.

Five months later, George Herman "Babe" Ruth was sold to the Boston Red Sox. On July 11, 1914, he played his first game as a major leaguer, pitching against the Cleveland Indians. He set a record in 1919 by hitting twenty-nine home runs for Boston. In 1920, his first season with the New York Yankees, he belted fifty-four out of the park. He led the Yankees to four World Series championships. By the time he died in 1948, he had hit an astonishing 714 home runs, including 60 in the 1927 season alone.

But it was in Fayetteville that "The Babe" first hit his stride. His first home run and first win as a professional pitcher both happened in North Carolina.

Rescue at Sea
·1918·

As the British tanker *Mirlo* left port on August 10, 1918, her captain tried to prepare himself mentally for the grueling hours ahead. He knew he was entering dangerous waters. At any moment, a German U-boat lurking below the surface could launch a torpedo at the *Mirlo*. Not only that, the Germans had strung mines across key shipping lanes, turning the churning sea into a death trap.

The world was at war. Thousands had already died at Tannenberg and the Marne, at Gallipoli and Vimy Ridge, at Verdun and Ypres. Bombs had fallen on the proud towns of Antwerp, London, Paris, and Karlsruhe. Battleships, destroyers, and submarines prowled the ocean, seeking enemy prey.

Although Americans fought in World War I, not a single battle took place on U.S. soil. Yet the U-boats the *Mirlo*'s captain feared that day in 1918 were not those menacing the waters off the coast of Europe.

The *Mirlo*, fully loaded with gasoline and kerosene, was steaming south from New Orleans into the Gulf of Mexico. In three days she would round the Florida Keys, and three days later she would pass Cape Hatteras on the coast of North Carolina. Kaiser Wilhelm of Germany and his military leaders had seen no reason to spare America's coastal waters, and U-boats and mines were an ever-present danger. The safest approach, the captain knew, was to travel about six miles offshore, close to the coastline.

Friday, August 16, found John Allen Midgett on duty at the Chicamacomico Lifesaving Station on Hatteras Island. In the morning, Midgett performed routine duties, running the engine of the power boat, inspecting all buildings, grounds, and apparatus, and conducting surfboat drills. The afternoon advanced slowly and uneventfully, then suddenly exploded—literally. Midgett's log entry at half past four o'clock that evening read:

> Lookout reported seeing a great mass of water shoot up in the air which seemed to cover the after portion of a steamer that was about seven miles E by S of this Station and heading in a Northerly direction, a great quantity of smoke rising from the after part of the Steamer was noticed but continuing her course for a few minutes when she swung around for the beach and then heading off shore, the fire was now seen to shoot up from the stern of the Steamer and heavy explosions were heard.

It was the *Mirlo*. The British vessel had been blown in half by mines, dumping tons of flaming oil and gas onto the water.

Midgett sounded the alarm. In record time, he and a five-man crew hit the water in Surfboat No. 1046, a vessel twenty-six feet long, made of juniper and white oak. High winds and heavy seas made it hard to pull away from the beach, but before too long, they were headed toward the wall of fire surrounding the burning ship. Midgett recorded the scene in his log:

> On arrival I found the sea a mass of wreckage and burning gas and oil, there were two great masses of flames about one hundred yards apart with the sea for many hundred yards in places covered with the burning gas. And in between the two great flames at times when the smoke would clear away a little, a life boat

could be seen bottom up with six men clinging to it, the heavy swell washing over the boat.

The surfboat's propeller kicked the sea into foam, cutting a narrow path as Midgett steered it through the intense heat, smoke, and fire. Underwater explosions belched up from below as the *Mirlo* went down. Flames singed the eyebrows of the men on the surfboat and blistered their skin. Pools of burning oil shifted constantly in the brisk wind, making safe navigation almost impossible.

Midgett and his crew pulled the six men into the surfboat then took two of the *Mirlo's* lifeboats in tow, one containing seventeen British men and the other, nineteen. "As fast as the men were landed they were carried to the station by my team of horses and the horse from station No. 180," Midgett later wrote. "I landed last trip at 9:00 P.M. and arrived at station at 11:00 P.M. myself and crew very tired. I furnished the Captain and all his crew who needed it medical aid, and then with some dry clothing, and their supper, and with a place to sleep."

Forty-two men were rescued from the *Mirlo*. For their efforts, the British government awarded the members of the surfboat crew Gold Lifesaving Medals. The U.S. government awarded them the Grand Crosses of the American Cross of Honor.

By the time the peace treaty was signed at Versailles in June 1919, World War I had sent nearly ten million people to their graves. Of these, about 126,000 were Americans. When history books list the Great War's battle theaters, they generally include the Western Front, the Dardanelles, the Eastern Front, the Balkan Front, and Mesopotamia. But the men who saw combat in those arenas were not the only ones who served. Far across the Atlantic, on the coast of North Carolina, John Allen Midgett, Zion S. Midgett, Arthur V. Midgett, Prochorus L. O'Neal, LeRoy Midgett, and Clarence E. Midgett fought a desperate battle for the lives of the *Mirlo* crew—and won.

The Case of the Telltale Ticket
· 1933 ·

"The criminal army in America today is on the march . . . . Crime is today sapping the spiritual and moral strength of America." These words could easily apply to modern times but, in fact, they were spoken in the 1930s by J. Edgar Hoover, head of the Federal Bureau of Investigation (FBI). He was referring to the activities of such infamous lawbreakers as John Dillinger, George "Machine Gun" Kelly, Charles "Pretty Boy" Floyd, and Lester M. Gillis (aka "Baby Face" Nelson).

During the 1930s, rural banks and post offices across the country were prime targets for marauding bands of hoodlums carrying sawed-off shotguns. State and local police struggled to cope with an unprecedented number of kidnappings, robberies, and homicides. Often the perpetrators of crimes in small towns were members of organized gangs headquartered in large cities like New York or Chicago.

Hollywood glamorized the role of crime-fighters in films like *G-Men*, starring James Cagney. In real life, however, there was precious little glamor involved. No one knew this better than Frank Littlejohn of Charlotte, North Carolina.

Born in 1885 near Gaffney, South Carolina, Littlejohn came to Charlotte in 1917 to run a shoe store. In the 1920s, he worked as an undercover federal agent to expose Ku Klux Klan activities. He was hired by the city council in 1927 to clean up prostitution in uptown Charlotte. The assignment was supposed to last thirty days, but Littlejohn remained on the police force for thirty years. By 1933, he had been promoted to chief of detectives. In November of that year he received a tip that "something big" was about to take place in Charlotte.

Although Littlejohn didn't know it, the "something" was connected to a man named Roger "The Terrible" Touhy. At the time Touhy was on trial in the Midwest for kidnapping. He had made his living as a bootlegger during Prohibition, selling alcohol to an impressive array of customers that included crime czar Alfonso "Scarface" Capone. Touhy claimed he had been framed for the kidnapping, but no matter how things turned out, he knew he would be paying criminally high legal fees for his defense. Where would he get the money?

On the morning of November 15, 1933, a mail truck was ambushed at the corner of Third and Graham streets in Charlotte. The bandits got away with more than $100,000 bound for the Federal Reserve Bank. Frank Littlejohn went to work. According to Roger Blackwelder, whose parents knew Frank and his wife very well, "Littlejohn . . . found a torn laundry receipt in a trash can near the scene of the crime. He pieced it together and traced it to Chicago."

The Chicago laundry ticket gave Littlejohn a valuable clue about the thieves: they had a connection to the Windy City. In less than two weeks he had the names of four suspects. Further investigation revealed that all four were connected to Roger Touhy. In his book *The Stolen Years*, published in 1959, Touhy described the Charlotte robbery's cast of characters:

> Blamed for the job—and guilty as a bank cashier with a credit rating in a gambling house—were Isaac "Ike" Costner, a Tennessee mountain whisky moonshiner, and Basil "The Owl" Banghart . . . Ice Wagon Connors probably was in on the Charlotte deal, too, but somebody tied him up with baling wire, shot him as full of holes as a Swiss cheese and deposited him in a muddy

ditch outside of Chicago before anything could be proved.

Another member of the Touhy gang, Dutch Schmidt, was also involved in the Charlotte caper. Schmidt got thirty-two years in prison for the crime. He and Costner wound up in the federal penitentiary at Leavenworth, Kansas. "The Owl" was already wanted for a wide variety of misdeeds. As Touhy put it "No matter what he said or did, the law was going to throw the key away on Banghart." According to Touhy, Banghart was sentenced to ninety-nine years in prison for previous crimes then sent to Charlotte where an additional thirty-two years were tacked on for the North Carolina mail heist. He landed in Menard Penitentiary in Illinois but did not remain there. A consummate escape artist, he had already managed to break out of prisons in Atlanta, South Bend, and Stateville. In attempting to escape from Menard, he wrecked a truck. According to Touhy:

> The federal government sent Banghart to Alcatraz, on the island in San Francisco Bay, to serve his time for the Charlotte mail robbery. Security was 100 percent for him there, unless he could steal a boat or a pair of water wings. Despite all his accomplishments, including flying airplanes, The Owl never had learned to swim.

Touhy himself was sent to prison for kidnapping, but his conviction was overturned years later when it was determined that key witnesses had lied under oath. Touhy had always maintained his innocence, and a judge eventually saw things his way.

Littlejohn recovered about twenty thousand dollars of the stolen money. The mail robbery was one of Charlotte's most spectacular crimes, and Littlejohn's efforts against "the criminal army" earned him a reputation at the national level. Described by some as "Charlotte's most outstanding police officer," he even caught the attention of J. Edgar Hoover, as noted by Roger Blackwelder: "He took pride in a personal letter from J. Edgar Hoover in which the FBI director referred to him as 'the finest detective in the United States.'"

Littlejohn's success in tracking down the Touhy gang also paved the way for his promotion to chief of police in Charlotte, a job he held until 1958. He died November 28, 1965.

The Last Shot of the Civil War
· 1941 ·

On December 7, 1941, Japanese planes attacked Pearl Harbor naval base in Hawaii. Eight American battleships and ten other naval vessels were sunk or badly damaged, almost two hundred American aircraft were destroyed, and nearly three thousand naval and military personnel were killed or wounded.

Twelve days later, Mrs. Virginia Humphrey, caretaker of Fort Macon State Park on North Carolina's Outer Banks, received some unexpected visitors: four U.S. Army officers. One of them introduced himself as Lieutenant Colonel Henry G. Fowler of the 244th Coast Artillery Regiment. Now that America was at war, he explained, it was essential that coastal waters be protected against attacks by Germany's fleet of submarines and surface navy. He informed Mrs. Humphrey that the Army needed to set up a military defense at Fort Macon.

She must have been astonished at the announcement. The fort was one hundred years old and had certainly seen better days. In April of 1862, during the War Between the States, it had been targeted by Union forces. Hopelessly surrounded and heavily bombarded by warships and artillery, Confederates holding the fort were forced to surrender. The fort remained in Yankee hands until the end of the war.

After serving as a civil and military prison in the late 1800s, Fort Macon was reactivated in 1898 for the Spanish-American War. Finally, in 1903, the U.S. Army completely abandoned the venerable but totally obsolete stronghold. In 1924, the federal government gave Fort Macon and surrounding land to the State of North Carolina for use as a public park.

Now Mrs. Humphrey was being told the state park would be closed down, and the building would be pressed into service as a battle station. The 244th Coast Artillery had originally been the Ninth New York National Guard. This fact did not escape the local press, which immediately pointed out that Fort Macon would soon be "occupied by Yankees" once again. No one guessed that the old relic would be a source of even richer irony before all was said and done.

Over a period of several days, Army vehicles loaded with men, supplies, and equipment rumbled down to the fort and Coast Guard station. Modifications were made, including running phone lines and electrical power lines and repairing leaks. By the time the move was complete, Fort Macon had about five to six hundred new tenants—an entire battalion, complete with head-quarters staff and support services. The guns were test fired and operational by December 24.

Paul Branch described the scene in an article for the Fall 1995 issue of the Fort Macon newsletter *Ramparts*:

> These were typical young men from the boroughs of New York City with accents that must have seemed as out of place to Carteret County citizens as the local brogue must have sounded to them. And the varied spectrum of unusual names of these men must have been a curiosity to the local folks, names such as Urbanski, Sczyerek, Chjonacki and Comacchio, which reflected their Russian, Italian, and Polish descent.

One incident in particular illustrated the "culture clash" especially well. Again according to Branch:

> Every night detachments of soldiers had to patrol the entire length of the beach to look for enemy landing

parties or raiders. One night a rowboat with two men came ashore. The soldiers questioned them and decided they might be enemies because of their broken English with a foreign-sounding accent. The two men were taken in for questioning but proved to be only local fishermen. The "foreign sounding" down east accent was just as unfamiliar to the soldiers as the New York–New Jersey accents of the soldiers were to the fishermen.

On January 1, 1942, the State of North Carolina officially turned Fort Macon State Park over to the federal government. A written agreement specified that the fort and park would be returned to the state once the war was over.

Knowing they would be stationed just two miles from Atlantic Beach, the "Yankees" might have hoped to spend some of their free time sunbathing. If so, they were doomed to disappointment. Beach or no, winters at Beaufort Harbor commonly featured blustery mixtures of rain, snow, and wind, with temperatures low enough to send a chill down the spines of Northerners and Southerners alike.

One damp, cold day shortly after the troops arrived, some of the men decided to build a fire in the fireplace of one of the rooms. They gathered kindling and logs but were not immediately able to find andirons to raise the firewood off the hearth. Soon, however, someone located the perfect thing: a pair of old cannonballs left over from the Civil War. Paul Branch tells what happened next:

> One of the cannonballs was a live shell, which quickly exploded in the fire in a room full of soldiers. Pvt. George Eastep remembered the blast went over him as he lay on his cot, but caught his bedding on fire. Shrapnel rattled against the opposite wall. One man was blown through a doorway into the adjoining room. By some miracle no one was killed.

According to Branch, Private Harry Chait required hospitalization due to burns suffered in the explosion and a couple of men had minor injuries. Later mentioned in "Ripley's Believe It or Not" newspaper column, the incident was described as "the last shot of the Civil War."

The men of the 244th Coast Artillery occupied Fort Macon for nine months before being sent overseas. They were replaced by other units. The Army continued to hold Fort Macon State Park until November 1944. At midnight on October 1, 1945, the park reverted to state control.

Today, Yankees who walk the grounds at Fort Macon are not on a "tour of duty" but a "tour of pleasure," soaking up history on North Carolina's Outer Banks.

A Rose Bowl By Any Other Name
· 1942 ·

O n December 8, 1941, the front page of every newspaper in America announced the same grim news: At a few minutes before eight o'clock in the morning of December 7, Japanese airplanes had attacked the United States naval base at Pearl Harbor in Hawaii. The United States had declared war on Japan.

Britain and France had been fighting Germany and its allies, Japan and Italy, since September of 1939. So far the United States had managed to maintain a neutral position, at least officially. That was no longer an option.

Even though war news dominated the headlines during the next few years, American reporters still found time to cover the more pleasant aspects of life in those days. The sports pages continued to tell of conflicts designed to entertain, not destroy.

Of all the contests waged on the country's playing fields each year, none drew more attention than the Rose Bowl, the "granddaddy" of college football games. The first Tournament of Roses took place in 1890, but football hadn't become a regular part of the festivities until 1916. Every year since then, the tournament had drawn a huge audience of spectators eager to see the nation's top teams compete. Whether it was Michigan against Stanford, Harvard against Oregon, or the University of Southern California against Pittsburgh, excitement and pageantry were guaranteed.

To handle the crowds, a 57,000-seat stadium was built in Pasadena, California. Christened the "Rose Bowl" by a local reporter, the stadium hosted its first Tournament of Roses game on January 1, 1923.

In December of 1941, readers of Raleigh, North Carolina's daily paper, the *News and Observer,* no doubt took time to check the latest news about the war. Many also turned to the sports section for an update on another topic of national interest: the Duke Blue Devils were scheduled to play the Oregon State Beavers in the Rose Bowl on January 1, 1942. Oregon State's season consisted of seven victories and two losses. Duke had gone undefeated in nine games.

Duke University, located in Durham, had sent its Blue Devils to the Rose Bowl once before, in 1939. They had lost a heartbreaker to the University of Southern California by a score of 7 to 3 when USC scored a touchdown with just forty seconds remaining on the clock. Duke's coach, Wallace Wade, was looking forward to a different outcome this time.

A great many North Carolinians shared his enthusiasm and made plans to travel across the country to watch the game. Ads in the *News and Observer* promoted an attractive offer from Southern Railway. A special train called "The Duke" would depart Raleigh on December 26. After stopping in Durham, Burlington, and Greensboro, it would arrive in Los Angeles on December 30. The return trip included stops in New Orleans, San Antonio, El Paso, and Mexico, as well as a visit to the Grand Canyon. First-class, roundtrip tickets could be purchased for just $126.74 apiece. Seats at the Rose Bowl were priced at $3.30 and $4.40, with boxes going for $5.50.

Excitement was in the air, but about halfway through December, the mighty winds of war threatened to knock the granddaddy of college football games off its feet. Fearing another attack by the Japanese, the U.S. Army requested that the New Year's Day parade and athletic contest be canceled. For a time, it appeared the clash between Duke and Oregon State would not take place.

Fans, players, and coaches alike were extremely disappointed by the Army's request. The 1942 Rose Bowl had promised to be an impressive contest. As Sam McDonald, sports writer for the *News and Observer*, put it:

> The Beavers are big and rugged and they have yielded only 33 points in nine games this season. . . . Duke's backfield shapes up better than Oregon State's, but the Beaver line may hold an edge.

> Tar Heels take their football seriously and they have taken this great Duke team to heart. It would be suicide for a native Tar Heel to predict anything except a Duke victory, but deep down inside these faithful Duke followers are afraid Oregon State may have a much better team than local fans will admit. But it will be a thrilling battle if the score is one-sided, close, or if there is no score at all. The crowd will make certain of that.

The *News and Observer* also reported the comments of Rube Samuelson, sports editor for the *Pasadena Post:* "I don't see the Blue Devils as heavy favorites," Samuelson said, "but I do believe they will win by two touchdowns. It's going to be a good game."

Oregon State coach Lon Stiner expressed a different view, repeatedly telling interviewers he could not understand how his team could be rated the underdog. "Everybody is going to be surprised," he said.

As it turned out, there was more than one surprise in store.

The game was not canceled. On Friday, January 1, a group of about three hundred college bandsmen marched to their seats at one end of the stadium. The crowd of fifty-five thousand fans grew more and more excited as both teams conducted their pregame exercises, supervised by coaches Wade and Stiner. Then the fun began.

Dick Dashiell, writing for the *Asheville Citizen*, offered a view from the sidelines:

Lon Stiner yelled his lungs out in warning, but the Blue Devils wouldn't believe him until about the second quarter of the ersatz Rose Bowl game this cold, gray afternoon. By that time, the Beavers from Oregon State had given authority to their coach's optimism, had got in the first blow and had gone ahead by a touchdown.

Elsewhere in the *Citizen* an even more colorful description appeared:

Oregon State's "orphans of the tall timber"—the bunch of kids who didn't have a chance—threw lightning through the mud and murk today to win the orphaned Rose Bowl game.

Cold, gray afternoon? Mud and murk? In Pasadena, California? Of course not.

When students of Tournament of Roses history journey back through time to 1942, they soon learn that Oregon State's 20 to 16 victory wasn't the only surprise provided by the Rose Bowl game that year. They discover why *News and Observer* sports writer Whitney Martin wrote:

A rose by any other name would smell as sweet. . . . In fact, although calling the contest the Humidor Game or the Pipe Bowl might seem more appropriate, the fact remains that to all practical purposes it still is the Rose Bowl game.

Due to the threat of enemy attack, Duke University offered to host the 1942 Rose Bowl. Oregon State accepted the offer, and the Army approved the location change. Southern Railway's special train "The Duke" never departed for Pasadena. The fifty-five thousand fans who cheered, gasped, and bellowed their way through the big game were sitting in Duke Stadium in Durham.

It comes as a surprise to most people to discover that on January 1, 1942, the Rose Bowl happened in North Carolina.

Showdown at
Torpedo Junction
· 1943 ·

A mild breeze stirred the surface of the water as the *Icarus* pulled away from Cape Hatteras, North Carolina, with eighteen-year-old John Ostensen at the helm. The day was warm, the ocean calm. It was about four o'clock on May 9, 1943, and weather conditions were perfect for a pleasure cruise. But Ostensen wasn't boating for enjoyment. He and the crew of the Coast Guard cutter *Icarus* had been ordered to hunt down and destroy the deadly "sea-wolves" lurking beneath the waves.

On December 8, 1941, following an attack by the Japanese on Pearl Harbor, the United States had officially entered World War II, siding with England, France, and Russia against Germany, Japan, and Italy. For the most part, the conflict was fought in Europe and the Pacific, but in January of 1942 Germany launched "Operation Drumbeat." Vessels traveling through waters off America's eastern seaboard were targeted by a fleet of German submarines or U-boats (a nickname derived from the German word for submarine—*unterseeboot,* meaning "under-sea-boat"). The Germans called a group of U-boats a "Rudel," meaning "pack" as in pack of wolves.

The Outer Banks of North Carolina became a danger zone. According to Sally G. Moore in an article for *The State* magazine:

> By early March the Germans realized they were in control. . . . From Hatteras to Lookout, almost every

night the residents along the coast would hear the explosions, and out over the ocean they could see the red glow in the night sky of one, two or three ships burning. . . . The residents didn't know what to expect and would not have been surprised at an invasion.

Over the centuries, storms off the coast of the Outer Banks had caused so many shipwrecks that the treacherous waters earned the grim nickname "Graveyard of the Atlantic." In the 1940s, as U-boats continued to sink allied tankers and cargo ships, the area became known as Torpedo Junction. More than fifty allied ships went down during the course of the war. Four U-boats were destroyed.

By the time John Ostensen took the wheel that mild day in May of 1942, the *Icarus* had already dropped several depth charges—drums filled with explosives set to go off at a certain depth. So far, they had not hit any U-boats.

To Ostensen, the term "sea-wolf" seemed appropriate given the way the sinister, steel-gray vessels traveled together, slinking along, stalking their prey. Even when they surfaced, their low silhouette gave them an appearance of innocence, like a wolf in sheep's clothing. Ostensen had no doubt that at least one sea-wolf was lurking nearby at this very moment. For the *Icarus*, the choice was clear: destroy or be destroyed.

Far below the tranquil waters, Kapitanleutnant Helmut Rathke watched and waited aboard U-352. In an article for *The State*, Gene Dees described Rathke's boat:

The grey tumescent submarine was 218 feet long and displaced 871 tons. She derived her power from a large six cylinder diesel engine when on the surface and a battery-driven electric engine when submerged. Her punch came from five twenty-one inch torpedo tubes. . . . Her crew consisted of 44 men, and she carried 14 torpedoes, each capable of sinking the largest ship on the ocean in 1941.

A native of East Prussia, Rathke had taken command of the U-352 in August of 1941, when the boat was first commissioned. He had not yet succeeded in sinking a ship and was hoping to have good fortune at Torpedo Junction.

After dropping more depth charges, the crew of the *Icarus* heard a huge explosion. Ostensen described the scene in a 1992 interview: "They [the U-352] shot a torpedo at us and it exploded in our wake. I thought I saw Old Faithful go up."

Looking through the submarine periscope, Rathke realized that the torpedo had failed to hit its target. His crew attempted to maneuver the U-boat into a better hiding place beneath the mud and bubbles of the explosion, but the *Icarus* responded quickly with a depth charge run, trapping Unterseeboot 352. In a 1992 interview, Ernst Kammerer, a midshipman on the German boat stated: "We blew up. All we could do is get out of the boat."

The *Icarus* continued to fire its machine guns after the U-boat surfaced to prevent any retaliation from the submarine's deck gun. Then the U-352 went under again for the last time. All was quiet. The Graveyard of the Atlantic had claimed another victim. According to Kammerer, the captain of the *Icarus* told the Germans, "I wish you a pleasant night" and left.

About thirty minutes later, the cutter returned to pick up the survivors. Now prisoners of war, the Germans were taken to Charleston, South Carolina.

Over the years John Ostensen had many opportunities to remember the incident, but one occasion in particular had a significant impact. In May of 1992, he returned to Cape Hatteras for a most unusual reunion. The *Wilmington Sunday Star-News* reported the event:

On Saturday, Mr. Ostensen and eight survivors of the German U-boat ventured into the graveyard of the

Atlantic Ocean to mark the 50th anniversary of their fateful meeting. About 15 Germans, including eight survivors of the U-352, and 10 *Icarus* crew members attended the ceremonies. ... Together they laid wreaths on the watery battlefield. Divers also placed a third one on the wreckage.

The First "Strictly Stock" Race

· 1949 ·

The midnight moon ducked behind a cloud as the driver of the 1933 Ford sedan pressed the accelerator, popped the clutch, and shifted into high gear. In spite of the darkness, he ran without headlights. He was racing against time—racing against the sunrise. Even more important, he was racing against the revenuer who had spotted him pulling out of a cove a few miles back. As he rounded a curve pushing ninety miles an hour, he knew only speed and skillful driving would keep his precious cargo of illegal whiskey out of the G-man's clutches, and his own self out of jail.

In hundreds of coves and hollows throughout the rural South, similar scenes were played out over and over again. In the 1930s, America suffered from an economic depression that threatened to snuff the very life out of her less fortunate citizens. Families needed food and clothing, and the makers of home-brewed whiskey paid their drivers well. What they didn't pay were taxes. Thus it was that along with local and state police, U.S. government agents, or G-men, often gave the moonshine haulers a run for their money.

But "all work and no play" would have made for a dull life. When moonshiners weren't barreling down the back roads with a load of whiskey, they were pitting their vehicles against each other in 'shine car competition. Insiders were of the distinct opinion that certain kinds of automobiles were better suited for the task than others. In his book *Flat-Out Racing*, D. Randy Riggs commented:

> While such machines [Ford V8, Buick, Packard] were fast and powerful, they were bulky and just couldn't be thrown around with the same wild abandon as the Fords. . . . Public Enemy Number One, Mr. (John) Dillinger even went so far as to write Henry Ford in 1934, "Hello old pal. You have a wonderful car. It's a treat to drive one." Clyde Barrow dropped Henry a note with yet another testimonial, "I have drove Fords exclusively when I could get away with one."

Eventually, from the basic need to earn a living, a unique form of entertainment evolved: stock car racing. One of the first people to realize the possibilities was Bill France Sr., a mechanic who lived in Daytona Beach, Florida. In the 1930s and the first half of the 1940s, he raced cars himself. He retired in 1946 to concentrate on a much larger dream: a national championship for stock cars. According to Don Hunter and Al Pearce in *The Illustrated History of Stock Car Racing*, "Big Bill" France insisted that all entrants in this championship race be "strictly stock class."

> France demanded it because he felt that Southern fans—and that was his primary audience at the time— preferred race cars that were similar to the street cars they could buy and drive. He knew his market, and Southerners of the late 1940s and early 1950s had virtually no interest in exotic, open-wheel, open-cockpit roadsters or Indy-type cars that were popular in other parts of the country. Many of the fans that France went after had served in World War II, and the second thing they wanted when they landed was a new car.

By 1945, when World War II came to an end, the grandstands at the Daytona Beach speedway were in sad shape. Four years of neglect during the war years had taken their toll. France checked around the Southeast and finally rented a dirt track in Charlotte, North Carolina. He began to promote a one-hundred-mile national championship race open to showroom stock cars only. The purse would be five thousand dollars, with two thousand dollars earmarked for the winner.

In order to be able to call his race a national championship, however, France needed a sanctioning body, rules, and point standings. When the American Automobile Association (AAA) declined to participate, "Big Bill" formed his own association: National Championship Stock Car Circuit, Inc. (NCSCC). He also created a slogan: "Where the fastest that run, run the fastest." The first-ever strictly stock race was scheduled for June of 1949. Southern-style stock car racing had entered a new era.

"Thirty-Three 'Pure' Stock Cars Race Here June 19," proclaimed a headline in the *Charlotte News*. The article explained:

> The race will be open to 1946 and later model cars, all American makes included except Jeeps, but qualifying tests must be made Thursday and Friday with mechanical inspections to be made Saturday. All cars will be inspected prior to the race.

"Charlotte Race Looks Like Family Affair," announced the *Asheville Citizen* on June 16, 1949, referring to the fact that two brother combinations, the Flocks and the Martins, were slated to compete in the race as well as one father-son combination, Frank and Archie Smith. By then the organization founded by Bill France had acquired a new name: National Association for Stock Car Auto Racing (NASCAR).

Qualifying trials were held on June 17 at the Charlotte speedway. The *Charlotte News* offered details about the entrants, which included automobiles made by Ford, Kaiser, Lincoln, Mercury, and

Chrysler. France was counting on a big turnout on race day, but even he was impressed when more than thirteen thousand paying customers swarmed into the seats. The roar that went up from the crowd at the drop of the checkered flag was music to his ears.

Bob Flock, one of three brothers in the pack, led the first five laps in a 1946 Hudson Hornet. The 1949 Lincoln of Bill Blair led laps 6 through 150. Hometowner Glenn Dunnaway led the rest of the way in a 1947 Ford and eventually beat Jim Roper's 1949 Lincoln by three laps.

Dunnaway's Number 25 Ford, owned by Hubert Westmoreland, had amazed officials with its smooth handling of the rutted turns, especially in the latter laps. Thousands of equally impressed fans left the speedway that day thinking Dunnaway had won. They were all in for a surprise.

An inspection following the race revealed that Dunnaway's car had altered rear springs, a clear violation of "strictly stock" rules. Dunnaway was eliminated, and first place was awarded to Jim Roper of Kansas. Following him were Fonty Flock of South Carolina; Red Byron of Georgia; Sam Rice of Virginia; and Georgia's Tim Flock, who recalled many years later, "Glenn Dunnaway won that first race at Charlotte in '49 and he was disqualified on account of he had helper springs that you put on to haul liquor."

The word on the track was that Westmoreland often used the vehicle to run moonshine. In fact, Tim Flock insisted that Number 25 had delivered a load the very morning of the race. True or not, the perception strengthened the legendary link between 'shine racing and sanctioned stock car competition. Westmoreland sued NASCAR for the two thousand dollars in prize money, but a judge ruled against him, stating that NASCAR had a right to make its own rules and enforce them. The other drivers put together a five-hundred-dollar "pot" for Dunnaway, who said he did not know the car had been altered.

In spite of the controversy surrounding the race's outcome, no one could deny that France had put together something extraordinary. Hunter and Pearce noted:

Under almost any criteria, that first Strictly Stock race was an unqualified success. . . . The purse was paid as advertised and the 13,000-plus fans proved to France and his staff that Strictly Stock (later to be named Grand National, then Winston Cup) might just succeed after all.

Succeed it did. In 1999, NASCAR's Coca Cola 600 race brought 185,000 fans to Lowe's Motor Speedway in Charlotte.

Today the Winston Cup Series consists of more than thirty races in which drivers earn points based on their performance in each contest. The person who accumulates the most points in a season walks away with an additional three million dollars, above and beyond any prize money earned from individual races. Such a figure is enough to bring a gleam to the eye of any Internal Revenue Service agent, especially since modern "revenuers" don't have to pursue the drivers around those treacherous curves to collect taxes owed. Instead, thanks to people like Big Bill France, they can sit back and relax with thousands of other fans and watch the "fastest cars that run, run the fastest."

Exposing "The Invisible Empire"
• 1953 •

W illard Cole of Columbus County, North Carolina, suddenly
sat up in bed, wide awake in the dead of night. At first he heard
only the pounding of his heart. Then his ears picked up the sound
that had roused him from sleep: someone was knocking on his
front door.

Cole's thoughts immediately flew to the note he had recently
received—a hate letter warning him that he would get some
"special medicine" if the opportunity presented itself. He knew
that might mean a brutal beating, a burning cross on his front lawn,
or worse. He thought about his children asleep in their beds. The
knock came again.

The Ku Klux Klan (KKK) had gone bankrupt in 1944.
Nevertheless, the organization was still alive in many areas of the
country, and in 1950, Willard Cole, a newspaper editor, decided
to give it the publicity it deserved. Linked to powerful families in
the Columbus County communities of Whiteville, Tabor City, and
Fair Bluff, the KKK even had law enforcement connections. Many
people felt it was useless to try to stop it. But Cole made a
commitment to fight "The Invisible Empire," as the Klan called
itself, through the pages of the *News Reporter*. In this effort he was
joined by Horace Carter, editor of the *Tabor City Tribune*.

Although Cole openly challenged the Klan with front-page
headlines and scathing editorials, he also quoted them and
presented their point of view. He figured readers would soon see

through the flag-waving and strident "Christianity" the KKK professed and into the poisonous core of the organization. Roman Catholics, Jews, and African Americans were at the top of their "hit list," but the Klan felt free to target anyone who violated their "moral" code.

The Ku Klux Klan first appeared in Tennessee in 1865. It was organized by former Confederate army officers who mistrusted and resented the activities of Reconstruction governments following the War Between the States. Its name was adapted from the Greek word *kuklos*, meaning "circle." The Klan initially vowed to "protect the weak, the innocent and the defenseless . . . to relieve the injured and oppressed; [and] to succor the suffering." Leaders were given titles such as Grand Wizard of the Empire, Grand Dragon of the Realm, Grand Titan of the Dominion, and Grand Cyclops of the Den. This first incarnation of the KKK was officially disbanded in 1869.

In 1915 the Klan was reborn in Georgia as a fraternal organization called The Invisible Empire, Knights of the Ku Klux Klan. By the mid-1920s, it boasted a membership of more than four million. In 1944, unable to pay back taxes owed to the federal government, the KKK disbanded. However, numerous independent units remained intact. Dressed in hooded robes to disguise their identities, Klansmen often attacked the innocent and defenseless—an ironic turn, given the fervent pledge of the 1865 Klan.

Initially many Columbus County residents were neutral or even sympathetic to the views of the KKK, which did a good job of tapping into deep-seated fears about communism and integration. The *News Reporter* had lost advertisers and subscribers since Cole had started his anti-Klan campaign. Yet he knew most of his neighbors were decent people with little or no tolerance for lawlessness. Sooner or later the tide would turn. He only hoped he would be alive to see it.

Sliding quietly out of bed Cole reached for his pistol. From the reports he had printed in his own newspaper, he knew members of the KKK wouldn't hesitate to use violence to make their point. His car had already been vandalized. He had put his children under a curfew at night for their own protection and had started carrying a gun to his office when he had to work late. It was especially disturbing to know that those who wanted to see him injured or killed had ties to local police. A call for help might be ignored.

The knocking had stopped. Cole approached the entrance to his home cautiously, gun in hand. He took a deep breath and jerked open the door. A dark, starless night stared back at him. No one was there.

As weeks passed, the phantom knocking was repeated several times at Cole's home on Clay Street; no one ever appeared. Things got a bit tense at the *News Reporter* late one night when Cole stuck his pistol in the face of staff member Jiggs Powers, who had entered quietly without announcing his presence.

Meanwhile, Cole continued to print both sides of the issue, letting the facts speak for themselves. On December 24, 1951, his editorial took the form of a letter to Santa Claus. He wrote:

If you, Dear Santa, have space in your pack, will you please leave all of us enough of the capacity to think clearly to enable us to understand that when the people run the government, there is mob violence; and when the government runs the people, there is dictatorship. Give us a package of common sense to maintain the balance in which we preserve our liberties and free enterprise and at the same time our cherished tradition of law and order.

In February of 1952, Cole's courageous crusade bore fruit. The Federal Bureau of Investigation (FBI) arrested ten Klansmen, including the former police chief of Fair Bluff and several former Tabor City police officers. They were charged with violation of civil rights and kidnapping.

"Ten Floggers Nabbed" read the *News Reporter's* front-page headline the next day. The article continued: "Operating in the cloud-darkened dawn of Saturday morning, between 35 and 40 FBI agents swooped across the Fair Bluff countryside."

Cole and his colleague Horace Carter had achieved their goal: to expose The Invisible Empire for what it really was and to hasten the end of its violent, lawless activities. This was the only reward they had sought, but not the only one they received. On May 5, 1953, the *News Reporter* won the Pulitzer Prize for Meritorious Public Service, one of journalism's most coveted awards. In October of 1996, a special Centennial Edition of the *News Reporter* stated: "Shared with Carter's *Tabor City Tribune*, the award had never before gone to a nondaily newspaper. Cole was 46, Carter, 32."

Writer and editor James Saxon Childers found Cole to be a singularly unpretentious individual. Following a meeting with him, he wrote:

[Willard Cole] was rather short and soft spoken. He had an easy smile. . . . In Cole's 8-by-10 office, the plaster was chipped and the chairs battered. Cobwebs drooped from the ceiling, and newspapers and books were splattered on an old metal frame. Cigarette ashes, tapped toward the tray, had skidded across the desk. Sometimes Cole would sit with one foot on a chair, sometimes with both feet on the desk. However he sat, he looked straight at you. Cole uses his Pulitzer Prize for a paper weight.

In 1992 Willard Cole was posthumously inducted into the North Carolina Journalism Hall of Fame at Chapel Hill.

Sitting in for Equality
· 1960 ·

At half past four o'clock in the afternoon of February 1, 1960, four young men entered Woolworth's five-and-dime store in Greensboro, North Carolina. They were dressed conservatively—two of them in suits and ties, the other two in knit shirts and dark slacks. All four wore long overcoats to ward off the winter chill. They purchased a few small items in the toiletries department then made their way to the lunch counter for a cup of coffee.

Although the men seemed calm, their presence clearly upset the waitress. She called the manager, who spoke briefly to the four then turned away. The men remained in their seats, but the waitress avoided them, never returning to take their order. When Woolworth's closed at half past five, the four unserved customers quietly put on their hats and left. The winter wind that blasted them as they stepped outside must have seemed temperate compared with the chilly reception they had received at the lunch counter.

After such treatment, most people would have vowed to take their business elsewhere, but the four freshmen from North Carolina Agricultural and Technical College (A&T) had a different approach in mind. Not only would they come back the next day, they would bring their friends. And they would keep returning until they got what they wanted: not just a cup of coffee, but acknowledgment that as paying customers, they had the right to be served at that lunch counter, regardless of the color of their skin.

Almost one hundred years earlier, President Abraham Lincoln had issued the Emancipation Proclamation, releasing slaves from bondage. In 1865, the Thirteenth Amendment was passed, abolishing slavery. The Fourteenth Amendment followed, giving African Americans citizenship and "equal protection of the laws." The Civil Rights Act of 1875 outlawed racial discrimination in hotels, public transport, places of amusement, and other facilities. At last it seemed the country was on track, moving ever closer to actualizing the lofty vision expressed in its Declaration of Independence: "All men are created equal."

Before long, however, the freedom train derailed. Julian Bond, an African-American legislator and historian, wrote:

Following the Civil War, the decade of Reconstruction represented the first and last use of full-scale federal power to protect the rights of black Americans. . . . Political compromises in Washington led to withdrawal of federal troops from the South. The rise of white terrorist organizations in the South erased Reconstruction's gains and the freedmen's protections, leaving them nearly defenseless. . . . By the end of the 19th century, black Southerners were returned to conditions that nearly equaled slavery.

Over the next several decades, progress was slow. During the 1950s, the United States Supreme Court ruled that public schools could not segregate students based on race, and Congress passed another civil rights act to protect the voting rights of African Americans. In spite of these efforts, in 1960 signs reading "whites only" were still all too easy to find in the "Land of the Free."

As the four African-American students from A&T left Woolworth's that February evening, they couldn't help thinking about the absurdity of their situation. They could purchase food or drinks in the store but could not sit at the counter to consume them. The manager had explained that this was "a local custom."

As far as the young men were concerned, it was a bad custom—one that needed to be abolished. According to Franklin McCain, who was one of the four students, "We had the confidence . . . of a Mack truck. . . . I probably felt better that day than I've ever felt in my life. I felt as though I had gained my manhood . . . and not only gained it, but . . . developed quite a lot of respect for it."

On Tuesday, February 2, McCain, Ezell Blair Jr., Joseph McNeil, and David Richmond returned to Woolworth's accompanied by twenty other students, including four African-American women from Bennett College. The *Greensboro Record* described the event:

> Today's group came in at 10:30 A.M. Each made a small purchase one counter over from the luncheon counter, then sat in groups of three or four as spaces became vacant. There was no disturbance and there appeared to be no conversation except among the groups. Some students pulled out books and appeared to be studying.

Once again the unwanted customers were told only whites could be served at the counter. Again they stayed until closing. They returned the next day and the next, their numbers increasing each time, until they occupied sixty-three of the sixty-five seats available. After four days, they overflowed into the S. H. Kress store, which also had a "whites only" lunch counter, down the street. By the end of the week, more than three hundred students—African American and white—were involved, along with a large crowd of supporters, hecklers, and journalists.

When asked what he thought about the process, Ezell Blair Jr. chose to take the long view, commenting:

> Some Negroes say we're moving, but not fast enough. I say that if it takes two or maybe three months to gain equal service with the white people in a chain store that

has a hundred years of history behind it, we've done something pretty big.

Soon the idea of the "sit-in" spread to other North Carolina cities. Students in Winston-Salem, Durham, Charlotte, Fayetteville, and Raleigh took up the cause. The movement continued through the spring, expanding into Virginia, Tennessee, and South Carolina.

In April, civil rights activist Ella Baker brought the sit-in leaders together in Raleigh, where she encouraged them to form a student organization that would be less centralized than established civil rights groups. Out of this meeting evolved the Student Nonviolent Coordinating Committee (SNCC). SNCC (pronounced "snick") was founded on the principles of racial equality, integration, and nonviolence.

Meanwhile, the unserved customers kept their seats at the Greensboro Woolworth's. Spring turned to summer, and still they remained. In his book *1001 Things Everyone Should Know About African American History*, Jeffrey C. Stewart wrote:

> The Greensboro students were cursed, spit on, and burned with cigarette butts by white youths, but maintained their sit-in until July 25, 1960, at 2:00 P.M., when, without prior notice, the four Black students were served.

In the end, it had taken the A&T freshmen almost six months to get a cup of coffee. Fortunately, they had accomplished much more than that, as historian William Powell noted in his book *North Carolina Through Four Centuries:*

> Similar activities by young blacks and others opened the state's theaters, hotels, motels, and restaurants to both races in 1963. . . . Protests such as the sit-ins, generally peaceful, succeeded not only in North Carolina where

they began but across the country as well. The Civil Rights Act of 1964 . . . prohibited discrimination in most public facilities.

Making
Medical History
· 1965 ·

As a salesman and furniture factory worker, twenty-six-year-old Robert Pennell of Hickory, North Carolina, had seen some hard times. Even tougher were the recent weeks he had spent in the Yadkin County Prison Camp serving three to five years for possession of burglary tools and breaking and entering.

It was June of 1965, three months into Pennell's sentence. As he took his place on the road gang working to clear a right-of-way near Lowgap, he wondered what could be worse than sweating and slaving all day under the scorching sun. He was about to find out.

Those who saw the accident later said Pennell stumbled and fell into a small hole. He stretched out his left arm to break his fall. At that exact moment, one of the other prisoners brought a bush ax down with full force, completely severing Pennell's hand at the wrist.

Few if any of the men working on the road gang would have called themselves squeamish, but they would not soon forget the gruesome sight they witnessed that day.

After applying a tourniquet made from a shoe string and a stick, guards rushed Pennell to Northern Surry Hospital in Mt. Airy. Dr. Ben Lawrence dressed the prisoner's wound then placed a call to Baptist Hospital in Winston-Salem, nearly forty miles away. In minutes he was connected with Dr. Jesse H. Meredith, general surgeon on the faculty of the Bowman Gray School of Medicine of Wake Forest University.

"Ben told me they had a young man whose hand had been amputated by a bush ax," recalled Dr. Meredith, a Mt. Airy native who had trained with Dr. Lawrence. "I told him to put the hand on ice and get the man and his hand to Baptist as quickly as possible."

Although Dr. Meredith gave his instructions with confidence, the truth was he had never reattached a hand. To the best of his knowledge, no one in the country had even attempted it. But Meredith, who was seen as something of a risk-taker by his contemporaries, held a basic belief: "Ignorance is the first enemy of judgment; fear is the second." He was determined that neither would impede his efforts to give Robert Pennell back his hand.

Experienced in several medical specialties, including heart surgery, orthopedics, transplants, and trauma medicine, Meredith was somewhat prepared for the type of operation he would be performing on Pennell. He was quite familiar with Dr. Ronald Malt's successful replantation of a boy's right arm, severed below the shoulder. That surgery, which occurred in 1962 at Massachusetts General Hospital in Boston, had been described in detail in the *Journal of the American Medical Association.* Shortly after reading the article, Dr. Meredith and his team began practicing microsurgical techniques.

"When Robert Pennell arrived, we told him that at the very worst, he would be left without a hand," Dr. Meredith said. "We advised him that we had never done this type of surgery before, which is about like telling someone you don't know how! He asked if anybody had ever done it, and I said 'Not to my knowledge.' He agreed to let us give it a try."

By noon on June 14, Robert Pennell was on the operating table. First, an orthopedic surgeon used two rods to connect the pale, limp hand to the forearm, stabilizing the wrist. Meredith knew it was critical to restore the flow of blood to the hand; otherwise, the tissues would die. He began by reconnecting the two main arteries that serve the hand.

"We had no surgical microscopes in those days," he said. "But we scrounged around until we found a little hood that had a magnifying glass on it. Normally, it was used to help people remove splinters."

Once the arteries were repaired, the tourniquet was released. Pennell's hand, which had been deadly white, suddenly blushed pink with life. Meredith knew the first significant hurdle had been cleared.

The surgical team next mobilized and repaired veins, deep tendons, and nerves, followed by superficial tendons and skin.

"Some of the procedures had to be designed as we went along, especially the artery techniques," said Meredith. "I had worked on the aorta during heart surgery, so I knew something about sewing arteries. During Pennell's operation, however, I realized I didn't know very much!"

Nevertheless, Meredith used his best judgment. As it turned out, he knew more than he thought he did. More than thirty years later, an article in the *Journal of the Southern Orthopedic Association* stated:

> Reading the description of this procedure in 1999, the management appears straightforward and out of a current textbook. . . . Intuitive reasoning led to the hand being placed on ice—now standard practice. Similar reasoning and a concern over toxic metabolic products prompted the surgical team to repair the arteries, allow hand perfusion before the venous return was reestablished, and then repair the venous structure. This practice prevented systemic toxicity, a complication of major limb replantation not reported until 10 years later.

Following Pennell's surgery, which took just over seven hours, Meredith elected not to put his patient in a cast. Instead, he had a physical therapist work with Pennell, getting him to move the tendons early, every day. Today such an approach is standard. In the 1960s, however, leading authorities on hand surgery were of the opinion that every repaired tendon should be immobilized for three weeks. Meredith had come to the conclusion that moving the tendons earlier would promote better function down the road by preventing adhesions. He was right.

Meanwhile, Robert Pennell received additional good news.

"He was pardoned and exonerated of his prison term," said Meredith. "They decided that was easier than trying to keep him under guard the whole time he was in the hospital. Later, he moved here to Winston-Salem and became a hospital volunteer."

Unfortunately, Pennell's newfound good fortune didn't last. On November 11, 1966, he was involved in an automobile accident. He suffered head and spinal cord injuries and died of complications of multiple trauma on November 24.

Having made major medical history, Dr. Meredith went on to complete several other hand replantations. In 1971, he developed the first kidney transplant program at the Bowman Gray/ Baptist Hospital Medical Center. He served as head of the medical center's burn unit and developed one of the first skin banks. He developed and taught the first course in North Carolina for the training of ambulance drivers.

Although he stopped performing surgery in 1993, Meredith continued as a member of the faculty at what is now Wake Forest University School of Medicine in Winston-Salem.

"As I tell my students, hindsight is very educational," he said in a 1999 interview. "But we have to learn to make judgments without hindsight and without fear. You don't want somebody who is scared to death flying your airplane or operating on you!"

It was that fearless approach that not only saved Robert Pennell's hand but also ushered in a new era in medical science.

The Prettiest Snow in One Hundred Years

· 1993 ·

During the month of March, weather in the mountains of western North Carolina tends to be a bit erratic or, some would say, "as wild as a March hare." The high temperature on a given day might be anywhere from thirty-three to seventy-three degrees Fahrenheit. Low temperatures range from fifty degrees all the way down to zero. Sun, rain, wind, and snow are all distinct possibilities.

No question about it, the region's inhabitants have been conditioned to expect the unexpected. Even so, Mother Nature always has a wide variety of tricks up her sleeve, many of them guaranteed to startle, astonish, and humble her audiences.

In early March of 1993, she no doubt raised an eyebrow in amusement when she heard residents of the mountain city of Asheville commenting on how little snow they had seen lately. Less than one inch had fallen during 1992. Just a little more than two inches had fallen in late February of the current year. So far, March was behaving very well. From a high of forty-three degrees on the fifth, the temperature had soared to seventy-three degrees on the tenth. Everybody knew winter wasn't quite over. Nobody imagined what lay in store.

On Wednesday, March 10, the *Asheville Citizen-Times* offered the following three-day forecast: "Thursday—High 54, Low 28—Partly sunny, not as mild; Friday—High 44, Low 34—Becoming cloudy, chillier, may be rain late; Saturday—High 40,

Low 30—Windy and cold with rain." Mother Nature chuckled and added a few more choice items to her cauldron.

By Friday, March 12, the *Citizen-Times* had revised its prediction for western North Carolina (WNC):

A low pressure center forming in the Gulf of Mexico is expected to strengthen before moving into Georgia on Saturday. Winter storms that pass through the gulf often make for WNC's heaviest snowfalls, especially when the front moves in over cold air. "All the ingredients are in place for a heavy snowfall," said Ron Jones, chief of the weather bureau at the Asheville Regional Airport.

Upon hearing the new forecast, Cataloochee Ski Area near Maggie Valley extended its anticipated closing date from March 14 to March 21. Things were looking good from their point of view. But the average citizen had trouble sharing the resort's enthusiasm.

"WNC braces for blizzard," announced the *Citizen-Times*. "Residents raid grocery stores."

Friday night, flurries began to fall. Within twenty-four hours, ten states along the East Coast had declared a state of emergency. On Saturday, March 12, for the first time in twenty years, post offices in western North Carolina failed to deliver mail.

"We haven't been able to deliver anything today," said the distribution manager at the central WNC mail facility. "There's not a way to get any vehicles out there in this mess."

The "mess" consisted of up to three feet of snow in the region's northern counties. Fifty inches fell at Mt. Mitchell. Parts of western North Carolina's two major interstates were closed. At least 200,000 North Carolina homes were without electrical power for days. Ashe-ville reported wind gusts of sixty-five miles per hour. On Saturday night, Flat Top Mountain in southeast Buncombe County recorded a temperature of nine degrees with winds of 101 miles per hour.

Overcoming all obstacles, a skeleton crew wrote, edited, and printed the Sunday *Citizen-Times* late Saturday night. Some of them hiked as much as three miles through knee-high snow to the newspaper office. The headlines they wrote told the story: "Storm of the Century"; "Like a hurricane with snow"; "Storm whips WNC."

Conditions were dangerous enough in the valleys, but even greater hazards threatened people in the higher elevations. Among them were hikers and campers who had unfortunately chosen the month of March to visit Great Smoky Mountains National Park, Nantahala National Park, and the Joyce Kilmer–Slickrock Wilderness Area. Frostbite and hypothermia were the chief complaints reported when they were finally rescued.

Stranded families called on every bit of ingenuity and courage they could muster. In Macon County, North Carolina, a young couple found themselves with no electricity, no usable firewood, no kerosene, and no water. Drifting snow had cut them off from help. With two small children depending on them, they did what they had to do—burning chairs in the woodstove and melting pots filled with snow for drinking water.

An expectant mother in Buncombe County went into labor at four o'clock in the morning on Saturday. She was transported to the hospital by a combination of farm tractor, rescue squad litter, and ambulance. The baby arrived safely at nine o'clock.

Many did not fare as well. An elderly woman in Madison County refused to be moved from her home Friday night. She was found dead Monday. Four Asheville residents and five Buncombe County residents were believed dead either as a result of the weather or because snow and ice slowed rescuers.

Acts of heroism were the norm. In the days following the storm, the *Citizen-Times* published a special column called "Snow Samaritans," containing vignettes that illustrated compassion and courage in the midst of disaster.

One rescue effort in particular caught the attention of *Citizen-Times* writer Dan Voorhis. During the height of the blizzard, a family called city communications to report that a man was having a heart attack. Two members of the Asheville Fire Department and two Buncombe County paramedics grabbed their jackets, baseball caps, and gloves and piled into the fire department's four-wheel-drive vehicle.

Snow was falling heavily. Forty-mile-per-hour winds were howling. The men managed to lurch and skid down Charlotte Street to a drift at the base of Cherokee Road. From there they started up the side of Town Mountain, hauling about seventy pounds of basic medical equipment. Voorhis described their ordeal:

The wind and cold were so intense that one of the men developed an ear infection and bronchitis and all experienced slurred speech, the first sign of hypothermia. One of the men barely dodged a falling power line knocked down by a cracked tree limb. . . . When they reached the house, they found [the heart attack victim] already dead and the rest of the situation grim. [His] 73-year-old wife, by now hysterical, and a neighbor had given him cardio-pulmonary resuscitation for 40 minutes, but had grown too exhausted to go on.

The four [rescuers] spent five hours at the house. First they calmed [the victim's] wife, trying to persuade her she didn't kill her husband when she stopped CPR. Then they tried to help her and her 96-year-old mother, who were alone in the house without any heat. They hauled in some firewood and lit a fire, shut the doors to the outer rooms to hold the heat. And rested up for the trip back.

In Highlands, sixteen patients had to be moved three miles down the road after power went out at the local hospital and generators could no longer sustain the medical center. Prior to the move, several physicians and staff members spent part of the night using a makeshift siphon to suck gas out of nearby cars to keep the hospital building warm and functioning.

By March 18, western North Carolina emergency operations were finally beginning to wind down. Although the damage from the blizzard was significant, in the final analysis most people seemed to feel it could have been worse. Newspapers paid tribute to those who worked around the clock to restore power or spent several nights and days in a row on the job at hospitals.

The resilience and positive attitudes that helped North Carolinians cope with Mother Nature's latest challenge were perhaps best exemplified by a centenarian living in north Asheville. Deprived of power and heat, she wrapped herself in sweaters and blankets, pulled her rocking chair over to the window and said, "This is the prettiest snow I've seen in one hundred years."

Her son built a fire in the fireplace, then prepared breakfast on Sterno heat. As the Sterno supply dwindled, he switched to cooking in an iron skillet on the fireplace embers. Eight meals later, the electricity was restored. His aged mother had only one comment: "It is still the prettiest snow I've seen in one hundred years."

Drama in the Real World
• 1999 •

Life in a fictional "television town" can be as eventful as scriptwriters care to make it. For example, take Episode 208 from the second season of *Dawson's Creek*, a Columbia TriStar coming-of-age drama about teens growing up in Capeside, Massachusetts:

"The Reluctant Hero"—CAN'T WIN FOR LOSING *(Originally Aired November 25, 1998, on The WB Television Network)*

Dawson's movie wins a prestigious film festival award, but his first major accomplishment as a filmmaker is overshadowed by the disintegration of his personal life, as Joey continues to pull away, his dad gets his own apartment and Jen spirals out of control. Meanwhile, Pacey has nowhere to go but up after his guidance counselor paints a bleak picture of his future, but in a moment of crisis, a newly focused and inspired Pacey rises to the occasion and proves that Andie's belief in him is well-founded.

During the 1998–1999 season, the residents of Capeside experienced few if any dull moments. Pacey, played by twenty-one-year-old Joshua Jackson, had to deal with everything from his abusive father to a complex relationship with Andie McPhee, a girl trying to hide the tragic truth about her family.

From the beginning, life in Capeside was considered "racy," "edgy," and "emotionally provocative." Viewers quickly gained intimate knowledge of the residents' lives. Capeside's streets became as familiar to them as their own backyards. The same was true for places regularly shown in the drama, like the video store, the jazz club, and The Ice House restaurant.

Before long, many of those who traveled to Capeside "by television" decided they would like to pay a real visit to the town. This was not a problem—assuming they charted their course for North Carolina instead of Massachusetts.

Wilmington, North Carolina "became" Capeside, Massachusetts, in 1997 when it was selected as a key location for *Dawson's Creek*. Creator Kevin Williamson based the drama on his real-life experiences as a young man in rural North Carolina.

Dawson's Creek fans soon learned that downtown Capeside was portrayed by the zero-hundred block of Market Street in Wilmington. The Ice House restaurant was also located in Wilmington, and the University of North Carolina at Wilmington doubled as Capeside High. In addition, the cast actually lived in Wilmington while the episodes were being filmed. Locals made up most of the crew and filled most guest roles and "extra" parts.

By the 1998–1999 season, crowds were gathering regularly to watch *Dawson's Creek* filming sessions. Thousands of fans from all over the world, most of them fifteen-year-old girls, began flocking to town to visit the places they had seen in the show.

As eventful as fictional life in Capeside could be, there was a moment in August of 1999 when Joshua Jackson discovered that real life in North Carolina could also be quite dramatic. Just months after fans watched his character, Pacey, act as a "reluctant hero" in Episode 208, Jackson played a starring role in an incident that might have been scripted like this:

SCENE ONE: Two young men walk along a beach. One carries a small surfboard known as a boogie board. They hear female voices shouting. Gazing out toward the sea, they see two people floating near the rock jetty that separates the inlet from the Atlantic Ocean. The men start to wave and return the greeting. They soon realize, however, that the women are calling for help. With only a second's hesitation, they dive into the water and begin to swim.

SCENE TWO: Reaching the jetty, the men find that one of the young women is having an asthma attack. She cannot get her breath. Gratefully, she clutches the boogie board offered by one of the men. Powerful waves rise and crash around the four swimmers. They struggle against currents created by the ebbing tide, unable to make any progress toward shore.

SCENE THREE: The young people continue to fight the riptide. It is clear they are growing fatigued. To their relief, a Coast Guard boat appears in the distance, making its way toward the group. In the nick of time, the four exhausted swimmers are pulled aboard.

Joshua Jackson was one of the men in this real-life episode. While walking along Wrightsville Beach on August 3, he and a friend noticed two "damsels in distress."

"Josh swam a boogie board to a girl having an asthma attack in the water," said Alan Serkin with the Wilmington Film Commission. "She was able to stay afloat with the aid of the board."

David Hartley, the show's coproducer, commented: "He pulled them out of the water, kept them safe and floating until the Coast Guard got there."

"*Dawson's* Jackson A Hero" proclaimed an article at Ultimate TV, a comprehensive online television site.

"How's this for a *Dawson's Creek* cliffhanger?" began a report from the Associated Press. The press release continued:

When Jackson and the other man reached the girls, powerful waves pushed them over the jetty and into the inlet, [Coast Guard Petty Officer Jody] Howey said. The falling tide prevented them from getting back to shore,

Howey said. A Coast Guard boat rescued the four about 7 P.M. No one was injured, Howey said.

"I'm so glad I was able to help out," said Jackson, according to Ultimate TV. "And I feel that anyone in that situation would have done the same thing." After the rescue, Joshua went back to work as Pacey Witter, odd man out and offbeat humorist of Capeside.

In the world of television, illusion is everything. A town in one country can be disguised as a city halfway around the world. Ordinary people appear larger than life, and their words and actions seem highly important. No doubt, on August 3, 1999, two swimmers were particularly willing to give up the illusion of Pacey Witter of Capeside, Massachusetts, in exchange for the very real presence of actor Joshua Jackson at Wrightsville Beach, North Carolina.

A Potpourri of North Carolina Facts

- The name "Carolina" was taken from "Carolus," the Latin word for Charles. North Carolina was named after England's King Charles I.

- North Carolina entered the Union on November 21, 1789. It was the twelfth of the original thirteen states.

- North Carolina's motto is *Esse quam videri* (To be rather than to seem).

- The state bird is the cardinal.

- The state tree is the longleaf pine, a source of resin, turpentine, and timber used by merchants and the navy for their ships.

- The state flower is the dogwood.

- The state song is "The Old North State" (words by William Gaston; music by Mrs. E. E. Randolph).

- At 6,684 feet above sea level, North Carolina's Mt. Mitchell is the tallest mountain in the eastern United States.

- North Carolinians announced their freedom from British rule more than a year before Thomas Jefferson drafted America's Declaration of Independence. In a document prepared in May of 1775, the citizens of Mecklenburg County declared themselves "a free and independent people," no longer ruled by the British crown.

- The North Carolina state flag has a blue field with two bars making up the fly, the top bar red and the bottom bar white. Centered on the blue field is a white five-pointed star. The gilt letters "N" and "C" appear on either side of the star. Gilt scrolls appear above and below the star. The upper scroll displays the date of the Mecklenburg Declaration of Independence, May 20, 1775. The date on the lower scroll is April 12, 1776, the date of the Halifax Resolves.

- The capital of North Carolina is Raleigh, named for Sir Walter Raleigh of England. Explorers commissioned by Raleigh were the first Europeans to visit the region that comprises present-day North Carolina.

- The University of North Carolina was the first public university to open in the United States.

- North Carolina contains one hundred counties.

- With an area of 53,821 square miles, North Carolina is the twenty-eighth largest state in the nation.

- In 1990, North Carolina had a population of 6,628,637 and ranked tenth among the states in population. The state has the largest American Indian population of any state east of the Mississippi.

- Elevations in North Carolina range from sea level along the Atlantic Ocean to 6,684 feet atop Mt. Mitchell in the western part of the state.

- Climate varies significantly within the state. The Coastal Plain and Piedmont Plateau regions experience mild winters. Hurricanes often strike the coast. In the Blue Ridge Mountains, winters are cold and summers cool.

- Farming dominated the economy of North Carolina until the 1920s, when it began to lag behind textile, furniture, and tobacco production. North Carolina now leads the nation in all three areas. Research Triangle Park near Raleigh is home to a large number of research and development concerns. In the western part of the state, handicrafts such as baskets and pottery are important products.

- The first Pepsi was created and served in New Bern, North Carolina, in 1898.

- Some famous North Carolinians include presidents Andrew Jackson, Andrew Johnson, and James K. Polk; public figures Dolley Madison, Reverend Billy Graham, Elizabeth Dole, and Sam Ervin; writers William Sidney Porter (O. Henry), Thomas Wolfe, and Clyde Edgerton; journalists David Brinkley, Charles Kurault, and Edward R. Murrow; entertainers and artists Andy Griffith, Thelonious Monk, John Coltrane, Howard Cosell, Rick Dees, Cecil B. DeMille, Roberta Flack, Ava Gardner, and Bob Timberlake; and athletes Charlie "Choo-Choo" Justice, Meadowlark Lemon, Sugar Ray Leonard, and Richard Petty.

- North Carolina has long been a popular movie filming location. One of the first pictures filmed in the state was *M'Liss*, based on a novel by Bret Harte. A silent western shot in 1915, *M'Liss* starred Barbara Tennant and Howard Eastabrook. More recently, in 1997, four movies shot in North Carolina topped the national box office charts: *Batman and Robin, Kiss the Girls, The Jackal,* and *I Know What You Did Last Summer.*

How North Carolina Got Its Nicknames

North Carolina is known both as the Old North State and the Tar Heel State.

When Carolina was divided in 1710, the southern part was called South Carolina and the northern, or older settlement, North Carolina. From this came the nickname the Old North State.

The origin of the nickname Tar Heel State has been more difficult to determine. According to historian William S. Powell, "The moniker is rooted in the state's earliest history, derived from the production of naval stores—tar, pitch and turpentine—extracted from the vast pine forests of the state."

The *Cincinnati Miscellany,* an Ohio journal published in 1845, referred to the people of North Carolina as "Tar Boilers." More than forty years later, poet Walt Whitman used the same term for North Carolinians. However, it was during the Civil War that the nickname Tar Heels began to be applied. Like Tar Boiler, it was a term of derision.

Walter Clark's *Histories of the Several Regiments from North Carolina in the Great War, 1861 to 1865,* published in 1901, attempts to explain the nickname by relating the following incident:

> In a fierce battle in Virginia, where their supporting column was driven from the field, North Carolina troops stood alone and fought successfully. The victorious troops were asked in a condescending tone by some Virginians who had retreated, "Any more tar down in the old North State, boys?"
>
> The response came quickly: "No, not a bit. Old Jeff's bought it all up."
>
> "Is that so? What is he going to do with it?" the Virginians asked.
>
> "He is going to put it on you'uns heels to make you stick better in the next fight."

According to historian William S. Powell, a San Francisco magazine called the *Overland Monthly* reported in its August 1869 issue:

> A story is related of a brigade of North Carolinians, who, in one of the great battles (Chancellorsville, if I remember correctly) failed to hold a certain hill, and were laughed at by the Mississippians for having forgotten to

tar their heels that morning. Hence originated their cant name "Tar Heels."

Even as the name was being used derisively by some, individuals and publications of the Old North State started identifying with the label, presenting it as a source of pride. In 1893, the students of the University of North Carolina founded a newspaper, calling it *The Tar Heel*.

By 1912 the nickname was recognized outside the state. The August 26 edition of the *New York Evening Post* identified Josephus Daniels and Thomas J. Pence as two Tar Heels holding important posts in Woodrow Wilson's campaign.

Bibliography

Poskito

Coe, Joffre Lanning. *Town Creek Indian Mound*. Chapel Hill, NC: The University of North Carolina Press, 1995.

"The Prehistory of North Carolina: A Basic Cultural Sequence," North Carolina Archaeology website. Last updated 12/7/99. (Reprinted with permission from *The Ligature*, NC Division of Archives and History [1980]. Revised 15 March 1996.) http://www. arch.dcr.state.nc.us/.

"Town Creek Indian Mound: A Reconstructed Indian Site," *The Heritage of Montgomery County, North Carolina*. Winston-Salem, NC: Montgomery County Historical Society in cooperation with Hunter Publishing Company, 1981.

Town Creek Indian Mound Guidebook. Division of Archives and History, Department of Cultural Resources, State of North Carolina. Edited by Linda Reeves. No publication date given.

Town Creek Indian Mound website. Copyright 1999 North Carolina Division of Archives and History. All rights reserved. Last Updated 10/19/99. http://www.ah.dcr.state.nc.us/sections/hs/ town/town.htm.

The Roanoke Colony

Barton, Lewis Randolph. *The Most Ironic Story in American History*. Charlotte, NC: Associated Printing Corporation, 1967.

Campbell, Elizabeth A. *The Carving on the Tree: A True Account of America's First Mystery—The Lost Colony of Roanoke Island*. Boston: Little, Brown and Company, 1968.

Durant, David N. *Ralegh's* [sic] *Lost Colony*. New York: Atheneum, 1981.

Explorations, Descriptions and Attempted Settlements of Carolina, 1584–1590. Edited by David Leroy Corbitt. Raleigh, NC: State Department of Archives and History, 1948.

The First Colonists: Documents on the Planting of the First English Settlements in North America 1584–1590. Edited by David B. Quinn and Alison M. Quinn. Raleigh: North Carolina Division of Archives and History, 1982.

Kupperman, Karen Ordahl. *Roanoke: The Abandoned Colony.* Totowa, NJ: Rowman and Allanheld, 1984.

Porter, Charles W. III. *Adventures to a New World: The Roanoke Colony, 1585–87.* Washington, DC: U.S. Government Printing Office, 1972.

Quinn, David Beers. *The Lost Colonists: Their Fortune and Probable Fate.* Raleigh: America's Four Hundredth Anniversary Committee, Division of Archives and History, North Carolina Department of Cultural Resources, 1984.

The Roanoke Voyages (1584–1590). Edited by David Beers Quinn for the Hakluyt Society. Cambridge, England: University Press, 1955.

Stick, David. *Roanoke Island: The Beginnings of English America.* Chapel Hill: University of North Carolina Press, 1983.

Blackbeard's Demise

Allen, W.C. *The Story of Our State, North Carolina.* Raleigh, NC: The Dixie Press, 1942.

"Blackbeard's Booty," The Insiders' Guide website. http://www.insiders.com/outerbanks/sb-ocracoke1.htm.

Blackbeard the Pirate homepage. Copyright 1999. Accessed June 13, 1999. http://blackb-eardthepirate.com/story.htm.

"Blackbeard the Pirate! And the Wreck of the Queen Anne's Revenge," North Carolina Maritime Museum website. Last updated August 29, 1997. http://www.ah.dcr.state.nc.us/sections/maritime/blackbrd.htm.

Garrison, Webb. *A Treasury of Carolina Tales.* Nashville, TN: Rutledge Hill Press, 1988.

Harris, Morgan H. *Hyde Yesterdays: A History of Hyde County.* Wilmington, NC: New Hanover Printing and Publishing, Inc., 1995.

Moore, John W. *History of North Carolina.* Raleigh, NC: Alfred Williams & Company, Publishers, 1880.

A Fight for Independence

"Battle of Alamance," North Carolina USGen Web website. http://www.rootsweb.com/~ncalaman/battleofalamance.html.

Cline, Lillian (teacher) and Elizabeth Black (director), eds. *A Short History of Cabarrus Country and Concord: Yesterday and Today.* (Sketches written by pupils of the sixth grade of Corbin Street Schools. Concord, NC, 1933.)

Fitch, William Edwards, M.D. *Some Neglected History of North Carolina.* New York: The Neale Publishing Company, 1905.

Hunter, C. L. *Sketches of Western North Carolina.* Baltimore: Regional Publishing Company, 1970.

Powell, William S. *The War of the Regulation and the Battle of Alamance, May 16, 1771.* North Carolina Division of Archives and History, 1976.

"The Regulator Movement and the Battle of Alamance," State Library of North Carolina website. http://statelibrary.dcr.state.nc.us/nc/ncsites/alamance.htm.

Sharpe, Bill. *A New Geography of North Carolina.* Vol. I. Raleigh: Sharpe Publishing Company, 1965.

Brother Against Brother

Carpenter, William L. "The Battle of Ramsour's Mill," *Lincoln County Heritage.* Lincolnton, NC: Lincoln County Heritage Book Committee, 1997.

Hoffman, Ray (local historian, Lincolnton, NC), Interview, November 1999.

A Pictorial Walk through Lincoln County. Published by Guy M. Leedy and compiled by Carolyn M. Stroup from a variety of sources, including the files of *The Lincoln Times-News.* Publication date not given.

"Struggle for the South," American Revolution homepage. http://ourworld.compuserve.com/homepages/ronmcgranahan/INDEX.HTM. Copyright Ronald W. McGranahan 1998–99, all rights reserved.

Wadsworth, E. W. "The Battle Site 200 Years Later," *The State,* May 1976.

A Golden Opportunity

Allen, W. C. *The Story of Our State, North Carolina*. Raleigh, NC: The Dixie Press, 1942.

Knapp, Richard F. *Golden Promise in the Piedmont: The Story of John Reed's Mine*. Raleigh, NC: Division of Archives and History, North Carolina Department of Cultural Resources, revised edition, 1999.

"Reed Gold Mine," State Library of North Carolina website. http://statelibrary.dcr.state.nc.us/nc/ncsites/gold.htm.

Rouse, John K. *North Carolina Picadillo*. Kannapolis, NC (self-published), 1966.

"Site of the First Documented Discovery of Gold in the United States," North Carolina Historical Sites website. http://www.ah.dcr.state.nc.us/sections/hs/reed/reed.htm.

The Story of Tsali

Arthur, John Preston. *Western North Carolina, A History, 1730–1913*. Spartanburg, SC: The Reprint Company, 1973. (Reproduced from a 1914 edition in the North Carolina Collection, University of North Carolina, Chapel Hill.)

Mooney, James. *History, Myths, and Sacred Formulas of the Cherokees*, containing the full texts of *Myths of the Cherokee* (1900) and *The Sacred Formulas of the Cherokees* (1891) as published by the Bureau of American Ethnology. Asheville, NC: Bright Mountain Books, 1992.

Parker, Mattie Erma. *Tar Heel Tales*. Raleigh, NC: State Department of Archives and History, 1946.

Powell, William. *North Carolina Through Four Centuries*. Chapel Hill: University of North Carolina Press, 1989.

Walser, Richard and Julia Montgomery Street. *North Carolina Parade: Stories of History and People*. Chapel Hill: University of North Carolina Press, 1966.

The Highest Peak in the East

Holshouser, Nick. "Elisha Mitchell and the Black Mountains of North Carolina." NCNatural website. Last updated 1/13/00. http://ncnatural.com/Resources/Adventure/Black-Mtns.html.

Schwarzkopf, S. Kent. *A History of Mt. Mitchell and the Black Mountains*. Raleigh, NC: Division of Archives and History, North Carolina Department of Cultural Resources, 1985.

Walser, Richard and Julia Montgomery Street. *North Carolina Parade: Stories of History and People*. Chapel Hill: University of North Carolina Press, 1966.

Webb, Chas. A. *Mount Mitchell and Dr. Elisha Mitchell*. Asheville, NC: The Asheville Citizen-Times Company, 1946.

The War in the Mountains

Alexander, Nancy. *Here Will I Dwell: The Story of Caldwell County*. 1956.

Histories of the Several Regiments and Battalions from North Carolina in the Great War 1861–65. Edited by Walter Clark. Originally published by *The State*; reprinted by Broadfoot Publishing Company, Wilmington, NC, 1996.

Jordan, W. T., Jr. "Sarah Malinda Pritchard Blalock." *Dictionary of North Carolina Biography*. Edited by William S. Powell, Vol. 5. Chapel Hill: University of North Carolina Press, 1994.

North Carolina Civil War Documentary. Edited by W. Buck Yearns and John G. Barrett. Chapel Hill: University of North Carolina Press, 1980.

Pearce, T. H. "Sam Blalock's Secret," *The State*, Vol. 42, No. 6. Raleigh, NC: State Magazine Printing Company, Inc. November 1974.

Powell, William. *North Carolina Through Four Centuries*. Chapel Hill: University of North Carolina Press, 1989.

Trotter, William R. *Bushwackers! The Civil War in North Carolina, Vol. II, The Mountains*. Greensboro, NC: Signal Research, Inc., 1988.

Scarcity and Speculation

North Carolina Civil War Documentary. Edited by W. Buck Yearns and John G. Barrett. Chapel Hill: University of North Carolina Press, 1980.

"A Female Raid," *Carolina Watchman*. March 23, 1863.

Skipper, Tom F. "A Female Raid," *The State*. Raleigh, NC: State Magazine Printing Company, Inc. June 1983.

The Stranger from New Orleans

Childs, Gladys. "The Pirate Who Came to Lincolnton," *The State*. Raleigh, NC: State Magazine Printing Company, Inc. September 1, 1971.

Geringer, Joseph, "Jean Lafitte: Gentleman Pirate of New Orleans," The Crime Library website. Dark Horse Multimedia, Inc. http://www.crimelibrary.com/americana/lafitte/main.htm, copyright 1999.

"Great Characters of New Orleans—Jean Lafitte, c. 1782–c. 1829," New Orleans Online website. http://www.neworleansonline.com/geno-lafitte.htm, copyright 1996–1999, New Orleans Tourism Marketing Corporation.

Hoffman, Ray (local historian, Lincolnton, NC). Interview, November 1999.

Keever, Elisie. "Lorenzo Ferrer/Jean Lafitte," *Lincoln County Heritage*. Lincolnton, NC: Lincoln County Heritage Book Committee, 1997.

Everything Is Dark

Ballard, Michael B. *A Long Shadow: Jefferson Davis and the Final Days of the Confederacy*. Jackson: University Press of Mississippi, 1986.

Clark, James C. *Last Train South: The Flight of the Confederate Government from Richmond.* Jefferson, NC: McFarland & Company, Incorporated, Publishers, 1984.

Harrison, Burton N. "The Capture of Jefferson Davis," *Century Magazine*. Vol. 27. Nov. 1883.

Mallory, Stephen R. "Last Days of the Confederate Government," *McClure's Magazine*. Vol. 16. December 1900.

Tate, Allen. *Jefferson Davis: His Rise and Fall*. New York: Minton, Balch & Company, 1929.

A King in His Pride

Chindahl, George L. *A History of the Circus in America*. Caldwell, ID: Caxton Printers, Ltd., 1959.

Conover, Richard E. *Give 'Em a John Robinson: A Documentary on the Old John Robinson Circus*. Xenia, OH: 1965.

"The Elephant Still Unmanageable," *Charlotte Observer*, October 1, 1880.

"Funeral of a Showman," *Charlotte Observer*, September 29, 1880.

John Robinson's Circus 100th Annual Tour, 1923.

John Robinson's Route: A Complete Compendium of the Tour and Incidents of John Robinson's Circus for the Season of 1901. Compiled and illustrated by Hugh F. Hoffman, press representative. Jersey City, NJ: Hoffman Brothers.

"A Mad Elephant," *Charlotte Observer*, September 28, 1880.

May, Earl Chapin. *The Circus: From Rome to Ringling*. New York: Dover Publications, Inc., 1963.

Nunn, Brian (elephant trainer). Telephone Interview, February 10, 2000.

Slout, William L. *Olympians of the Sawdust Circle: A Biographical Dictionary of the Nineteenth Century American Circus*. San Bernardino, California: Borgo Press, 1998.

Smith, "Elephant George." E-mail correspondence, February 2000.

"This Last and Most Wonderful Discovery of the Century"

"At the Hospital," *Charlotte Daily Observer*, January 11, 1898, p. 6.

"Davidson Students in 1896 Stumbled On History Making X-Ray Discoveries," *Charlotte Observer*, December 9, 1949.

"He Found It," *Daily Concord Standard*, January 7, 1898, p. 1.

"The Operation Successful," *Charlotte Daily Observer*, January 9, 1898, p. 6.

Presbyterian Hospital, The Spirit of Caring, 1903–1985. Dallas, Texas: Taylor Publishing Company. Copyright 1991 by Presbyterian Hospital.

"Second X-Ray Operation," *Charlotte Daily Observer*, January 13, 1898, p. 6.

"A Successful Operation," *Daily Concord Standard*, January 10, 1898, p. 3.

"Thimble Found By The X-Ray," *Charlotte Daily Observer*, January 8, 1898, p. 5.

"The X-ray Century," Perry Sprawls, Ph.D., Editor, Emory University website. http://www.cc.emory.edu/X_RAYS/century_06.htm.

"X-Rays," *Charlotte Daily Observer*, January 25, 1898, p. 5.

"X-Rays Locate a Pin," *Charlotte Daily Observer*, January 12, 1898, p. 6.

Flight of Fancy

Geibert, Ronald R. and Patrick B. Nolan. *Kitty Hawk and Beyond: The Wright Brothers and the Early Years of Aviation, A Photographic History.* Dayton, OH: Wright State University Press, 1990.

Walsh, John Evangelist. *One Day at Kitty Hawk.* New York: Thomas Y. Crowell Company, 1975.

Wescott, Lynanne and Paula Degen. *Wind and Sand: The Story of the Wright Brothers at Kitty Hawk.* New York: Harry N. Abrams, Inc., Publishers, 1983.

"Wright Brothers National Memorial," State Library of North Carolina website, North Carolina Encyclopedia, Historic Sites. http://statelibrary.dcr.state.nc.us/nc/cover.htm. Reviewed 7/97.

Wright Brothers National Memorial website. U.S. Department of the Interior, National Park Service. http://www.nps.gov/wrbr/wright.htm. Accessed August 1999.

Wright, Orville and Wilbur. "The Wright Brothers Aeroplane," *Century Magazine*, September 1908. Posted by Gary Bradshaw. http://www.wam.umd.edu/~stwright/WrBr/Wrights.html.

Batter Up!

"The Official Web Site of Babe Ruth," CMG Worldwide. http://www.baberuth.com.

Creamer, Robert W. *Babe: The Legend Comes to Life.* New York: Simon & Schuster, 1974.

Skipper, Tom F. "Babe Ruth in North Carolina," *The State*. Vol. 52, No. 12. Raleigh, NC: State Magazine Printing Company, Inc., May 1985.

Stevens, Tim. "Babe's Batboy Remembers That First Home Run," *The State*, Vol. 48, No. 7. Raleigh: State Magazine Printing Company, Inc., December 1980.

Rescue at Sea

Chicamacomico Lifesaving Station website. http://www.hatteras-nc.com/chicamacomico/.

"Famed boat restored for historical display," newspaper article provided by Robert Huggett, Chicamacomico Historical Association, Inc., Rodanthe, NC.

Midgett, John A. Transcript of Chicamacomico Coast Guard Station Log, August 16, 1918.

The Case of the Telltale Ticket

Blackwelder, Roger. "This Officer Was Also a Gentleman, As Well As A Pal." *Charlotte Observer*, February 28, 1999.

Harkey, W. Hugh. *More Tales from the Hornet's Nest*. Charlotte, NC: Hornet's Nest Productions, 1992.

Touhy, Roger (with Ray Brennan). *The Stolen Years*. Cleveland: The Pennington Press, Inc. 1959.

The Last Shot of the Civil War

Branch, Paul. "Yankees Reoccupy Fort Macon" and "World War II Comes to Ft. Macon." *Ramparts*. Fall 1995. Posted on Fort Macon Ramparts website. http://www.clis.com/friends/default.htm.

Fort Macon State Park website. http://ils.unc.edu/parkproject/foma.html.

A Rose Bowl By Any Other Name

"Army Asks Cancellation of Pasadena's Rose Bowl," *News and Observer*, Raleigh, NC, December 14, 1941.

"Beavers' Don Durdan Is Great," *Asheville Citizen*, Asheville, NC, January 1, 1942.

"Everyone Writes About Rose Bowl," *News and Observer*, Raleigh, NC, December 18, 1941.

"Oregon State Accepts Bid to Play Devils at Durham," *News and Observer*, Raleigh, NC, December 16, 1941.

"Oregon State Wins Over Duke 20 to 16 in Rose Bowl Game," *Asheville Citizen*, Asheville, NC, January 2, 1942.

"The Rose Bowl Game History," Tournament of Roses website. http://www.tournamentofroses.com

"Rose Bowl Special Train 'The Duke' Will Leave December 26, 1941," *News and Observer*, Raleigh, NC, December 9, 1941.

"Today Is the Day for Rose Bowl Battle," *News and Observer*, Raleigh, NC, January 1, 1942.

Showdown at Torpedo Junction

Dees, Gene. "Where a Sea Wolf Died," *The State*. Raleigh, NC: State Magazine Printing Co., Inc. January 1984.

Moore, Sallie G. "When the U-Boats Hit Cape Lookout," *The State*. Raleigh, NC: State Magazine Printing Co., Inc. April 15, 1968.

"One Last Word," *The State*. Raleigh, NC: State Magazine Printing Co., Inc. July 1978.

Powell, William. *North Carolina Through Four Centuries*. Chapel Hill: University of North Carolina Press, 1989.

Shaw, Andrea. "Sinking Off N.C. Coast Remembered." *Wilmington Sunday Star-News*. May 10, 1992.

The First "Strictly Stock" Race

"Charlotte Race Looks Like Family Affair," *Asheville Citizen*, June 16, 1949.

"Dunnaway Gets $500," *Charlotte News*, June 24, 1949.

"Dunnaway Is Disqualified, Roper Winner," *Charlotte News*, June 20, 1949.

"Father and Son Enter Cars for Race Sunday," *Charlotte News*, June 15, 1949.

Hunter, Don and Al Pearce. *The Illustrated History of Stock Car Racing*. Osceola, WI: MBI Publishing Company, 1998.

Lowe's Motor Speedway 1999 Event Attendance Summary.

Riggs, D. Randy. *Flat-Out Racing: An Insider's Look at the World of Stock Cars*. New York: MetroBooks, 1995.

"Thirty-Three 'Pure' Stock Cars Race Here June 19," *Charlotte News*, June 9, 1949.

"Thirty-Three Scheduled For Stock Trials Today," *Charlotte News*, June 17, 1949.

Exposing "The Invisible Empire"

Hinnant, Lee. "Brave Editor Willard Cole Took on the Ku Klux Klan," *News Reporter,* Centennial Edition, October, 1996.

"Ku Klux Klan." Compton's Encyclopedia Online. http://www. optonline.com/.

"Ku Klux Klan." Funk & Wagnalls Online. http://www.funkand wagnalls.com/.

Sitting in for Equality

Ashmore, Harry S. *Civil Rights and Wrongs: A Memoir of Race and Politics, 1944–1994.* New York: Pantheon Books, 1994.

Levine, Michael L. *African Americans and Civil Rights from 1619 to the Present.* Phoenix, Oryx Press, 1996.

Powell, William. *North Carolina Through Four Centuries.* Chapel Hill: University of North Carolina Press, 1989.

Stewart, Jeffrey C. *1001 Things Everyone Should Know About African American History.* New York: Doubleday, 1996.

Wexler, Sanford. *The Civil Rights Movement: An Eyewitness History.* New York: Facts on File, Inc., 1993.

Making Medical History

Meredith, Jesse H., M.D. Telephone interview, November 23, 1999.

Meredith, Jesse H., M.D., and L. Andrew Koman, M.D. "Replantation of Completely Amputated Distal Forearm—1965," *Journal of the Southern Orthopedic Association*, Vol. 8, No. 3, Fall 1999.

Nomination of Dr. Jesse H. Meredith for the North Carolina Award for Public Service (text of speech, provided by Bob Conn, Public Relations, Wake Forest School of Medicine), February 18, 1991.

"Rejoined Hand, Arm May Work," *Winston-Salem Journal*, June 16, 1965.

"Severed Hand Back, Outlook 'Pretty Good,'" *Asheville Citizen*, June 16, 1965.

The Prettiest Snow in One Hundred Years

Alexander, Phil, "Snow Expected Over mountains This Weekend," *Asheville Citizen-Times*, March 12, 1993.

Alexander, Phil, "Hospital Workers Brave Weather, Roads to Move," *Asheville Citizen-Times*, March 21, 1993.

"Baby Born in Midst of Blizzard," *Asheville Citizen-Times*, March 20, 1993.

CLIMVIS National Weather Service website. http://www.ncdc.noaa.gov.

Dryman, Susan, "Blizzard of 1936 Caught All Unaware," *Asheville Citizen-Times*, March 15, 1993.

"East Coast Blizzard" information box, *Asheville Citizen-Times*, March 14, 1993.

"It Was the Prettiest Snow Ever," *Asheville Citizen-Times*, March 23, 1993.

Morrison, Clarke, "Relief Effort Gears Down," *Asheville Citizen-Times*, March 20, 1993.

Sandford, Jason, and Bob Scott, "More Missing Hikers Found; Search Continues for 24 Teens," *Asheville Citizen-Times*, March 16, 1993.

Scott, Bob, "Macon Family Burns Furniture to Stay Warm in Blizzard of '93," *Asheville Citizen-Times*, March 22, 1993.

"Sunday *Citizen-Times* Publishes Despite Storm," *Asheville Citizen-Times*, March 14, 1993.

Voorhis, Dan, "Storm Whips WNC," *Asheville Citizen-Times*, March 14, 1993.

"WNC Braces for Blizzard," *Asheville Citizen-Times*, March 12, 1993.

Drama in the Real World

Comer, Susan L., "Behind the Scenes: *Dawson's Creek*," *Our State*, April 1999.

"*Dawson's Creek* Creating a Buzz," Associated Press, 1998.

"*Dawson's Creek* Star, Three Others Pulled from Masonboro Inlet," Associated Press, 1999.

Dawson's Creek website, http://www.dawsonscreek.com/.

"*Dawson's* Jackson a Hero," August 4, 1999, Ultimate TV, http://www.UltimateTV.com/corporate.

Digital Dawson website, http://www.geocities.com/TelevisionCity/Stage/8130/dd.html.

Lamb, Dawn (owner, The Ice House, Wilmington, NC), telephone interview, July 27, 1999.

McEntire, Torri, "*Dawson's Creek*—Sweaty Palms, Holding Hands, the First Kiss," Ultimate TV website, http://www.ultimatetv.com/.

McFadden, Kay, "*Dawson's Creek* Frankly, Lovingly Presents Teen Coming of Age," *Seattle Times* website, http://www.seattletimes.com.

Serkin, Alan (Wilmington Regional Film Commission). Telephone interview, July 16, 1999.

Serkin, Alan (Wilmington Regional Film Commission). E-mail correspondence, September 24, 1999.

The WB—*Dawson's Creek* website, copyright The Warner Bros. Television Network 1998, http://www.dawsons-creek.com/.

A Potpourri of North Carolina Facts

Official North Carolina Website—North Carolina Kids Page (a publication of the North Carolina Secretary of State's office). http://www.state.nc.us/secstate/kidspg/famous.htm.

"North Carolina," Funk and Wagnalls website, http://www.funkandwagnalls.com, copyright 1999, Versaware, Inc.

Powell, William S. "What's in a Name?" *Tar Heel* magazine, Cygnet Communications Company, March 1982, reprinted and distributed by North Carolina Collection, University of North Carolina Library, Chapel Hill, NC.

Index

About the Author

Born in Illinois, Scotti McAuliff Kent spent the first twenty-six years of her life in the Midwest. She moved to the mountains of western North Carolina in 1977 and lived there for more than twenty years before moving back to Illinois at the turn of the new century.

A freelance writer specializing in health care as well as North Carolina history, Scotti also enjoys music, cats, astrology, travel, and writing fiction for middle-grade and young adult readers.

Acknowledgments

I am profoundly grateful to the following people, who shared with me their time, knowledge, and experiences:

- Steve Gossard, Circus Historian, Illinois State University
- Gudmundur Helgason of Iceland, creator of the "uboat.net" website
- Les High, Managing Editor, *The News Reporter*, Whiteville, NC
- Ray Hoffman, Lincolnton, NC
- Robert Huggett, Chicamacomico Historical Association, Inc., Rodanthe, NC
- Teresa Thomason, Special Collections, Illinois State University
- Tim Treadwell, NCNatural website
- Bernice Zimmer, Circus World Museum, Baraboo WI

I also appreciate everyone who agreed to be interviewed about a specific subject. They are mentioned by name in the appropriate sections of the book.

My special thanks to Lew Powell, author of *On This Day in North Carolina*, for giving me such an excellent foundation on which to build my chapters; and to my editor, Charlene Patterson, for her enthusiasm and perceptiveness.